Holding to an unseen hand

Secrets Revealed in the Shadows of Life

Second edition
INCLUDES 6 NEW DEVOTIONALS!

Donna Lott

Holding to an Unseen Hand

Secrets Revealed in the Shadows of Life

Donna Lott

Published by Light and Laughter Ministries
2191 Woodbriar Dr.
Buford, GA 30518
www.donnalott.com

ISBN 978-1976464041

Acknowledgements

With sincere appreciation and gratitude, I must give credit to the many wonderful friends and family members who have helped make the writing of this book possible. Some of you may very well recognize yourselves as the inspiration for one or more of the entries recorded here. To you, thank you for the rich blessing you are to me.

Also, to my precious writers' group, your passion for writing is nothing short of contagious. You have graciously persevered with me through the years and have been a constant and consistent source of accountability and love.

I want to recognize my sweet speaking mentor, friend and funny lady, Frankie D. Sherman. Your phone calls and emails are a joy. Thank you for letting me lean on you for ministry advice and counsel.

A special word of thankfulness goes to my husband, Don, who, when I was first diagnosed with RP, told me it would be a pleasure to be my eyes someday. He has proved himself faithful to that promise through his work on this book, and in countless other ways.

In addition I would like to give kudos to my friends and prayer partners – you know who you are. I couldn't make it through life without you – book or not.

Lastly, an extreme debt of gratitude goes to my editor, Gloria Spencer, who worked passionately and tirelessly to make this book the best it could be.

To My husband, Don,
our three sons, Nathan, Benjamin and Stephen,
and my mom, Annie.

Introduction To The Second Edition

I have always been a people person but when God called me to launch a speaking ministry, I was frightened yet more than a little excited. Now, I can't imagine doing anything else.

I love speaking at retreats, conferences, and other special events. Something unexplainable happens every time we gather together with the express purpose of spending time with each other and with the Lord. When we unplug from the world and plunge into His word, when we power off electronically and power up spiritually and when we turn off external distractions in order to tune into the internal voice of the Spirit, God shows up every time and He speaks.

God has richly blessed me every time He has allowed me to step onto the platform and then afterward to meet personally with His beloveds. I am moved by their individual stories and I cherish moments at the altar or at the book table. I have met so many new friends and have had the honor of laughing with, crying with, and praying with them.

I first wrote *Holding to an Unseen Hand* in response to the requests of speaking audiences. Now I am releasing this devotional with a new cover design, six new devotionals and a compilation of some of my most-treasured Scripture passages.

I hope you will enjoy *Holding to an Unseen Hand* more than ever and I hope you will contact me to share what the Lord is doing in your life.

So then, just as you received Christ Jesus as Lord, continue to live your lives in him, rooted and built up in him, strengthened in the faith as you were taught, and overflowing with thankfulness.
Colossians 2:6-7

Always yours,

Donna
contact@donnalott.com

Personal Note from Donna

More Faith than a Mustard Seed

If you have faith as small as a mustard seed,
you can say to this mountain,
"Move from here to there" and it will move.
Nothing will be impossible for you.
Matthew 17:20

What was wrong with me anyway?

I'd been a believer for decades, so why was I struggling to trust God? Hadn't He been the one to carry me through the challenges associated with earning a college degree, building a marriage, and having children? I had believed Him all those years through job losses, financial strains, illnesses, and rejections of various kinds. Why, then, so little faith just when I needed it most?

I was a twenty-eight-year-old wife and mother of two when I received shocking news that rattled me to the core. I had gone for a routine eye exam expecting to receive a new contact prescription. Instead, I was referred to a retina specialist. At the end of a very long day of eye charts, drops, and tests, the doctor told me, "You'll most likely be blind someday."

The diagnosis of retinitis pigmentosa, the prognosis of complete blindness, and subsequent changes in my vision sent me reeling. My faith took a nosedive and I spiraled downward at breakneck speed.

Me—blind someday? This couldn't be happening to me! I protested with each noticeable change in my eyesight. As the deterioration continued, I wanted desperately to be strong and courageous, to exhibit the kind of belief that could do the impossible, move-that-mountain kind of faith. Honestly, though, I was exerting myself to muster even a mustard seed of faith. Before my diagnosis there had been weeks when I barely cleared the hurdles of HUGGIES®, hormones, and hat-hair. How in the world would I survive the world of vision loss?

Oddly enough, as a born-again Christian, I was in a real quandary. You see, I trusted Jesus to take me to heaven, so why couldn't I trust Him to take me through the day-to-day struggles of vision loss? In my crisis I came face to face with the "ye" of the familiar quote, "O ye of little faith." I found that the *ye* was indeed *me!*

What was a nice Christian gal like me doing in a doubt-filled place like this? Better yet, what was a girl to do about it? What are any of us to do when our faith falters?

For me, it was a matter of eventually realizing that although the doctors had identified a problem with my vision, the more debilitating problem in my life was one of focus. The writer of Hebrews exhorts us we are to be "fixing our eyes on Jesus, the author and perfecter of our faith" (Hebrews 12:2 NASB). The Father led me to see—through the counsel of His Holy Spirit, the Scriptures, and dear Christian friends—that the key to growing in faith in spite of the challenges I faced was keeping my eyes fixed firmly on Jesus.

What about you? Are your eyes fixed on Jesus, the author and perfecter of your faith?

This devotional guide is designed to help shift your focus to Jesus. If your life, like mine, is characterized by heartaches, hurdles, and hardships, my hope and prayer is that this little book will encourage you. My desire is that together we will grow to know God better and love Him more. Each day's entry includes powerful words from the Bible, a few personal thoughts from my own faith-walk, and a prayer. I believe you will grow in faith as you spend precious time with God.

The Lord has been my faithful friend and guide. I often say it took facing blindness for God to really open my eyes. As my sight fades, God is giving me more faith than a mustard seed. He is teaching me to hold to His unseen hand as He reveals secrets in the shadows of life. I know He will do the same for you.

Jesus promised we could move mountains with just a little faith. Imagine what can happen when we set our eyes firmly on Him.

"Let it be, Sweet Jesus. Let it be."

With great love for you,

Donna

Week One

Monday
Holding to an Unseen Hand

Let us hold unswervingly to the hope we profess,
for he who promised is faithful.
Hebrews 10:23

My faith-walk began when I was about ten or so.

On that hot July morning I was sitting on a pew in our little country church. I'd enjoyed, as always, singing the songs I loved so much from the old Baptist Red Hymnal. When the song service ended the visiting preacher took his place in the pulpit. I listened offhandedly to his opening few sentences. He hadn't even opened the Bible yet when God got my attention. The Lord's unseen hand tapped me on the spiritual shoulder. He whispered in my spiritual ear and I knew that day's sermon was meant for me.

I sat up on the pew a little straighter and listened more closely. While the voice of the preacher sounded out through the congregation, the voice of God spoke to my heart. He turned on a spiritual light and awakened my soul to the truth of the message. The Holy Spirit convinced me that the "sinner in need of forgiveness" was me. My heart pounded in my chest as I came into deeper understanding that the Word was not as much about transferring information as it was about a total transformation—mine, that is.

Throughout the service the Lord seemed to say, "Today is the day. It's time. Repent and believe."

At the end of the service when everyone began to sing, I felt an urging I'd never felt before. God was calling me to follow Him. His voice spoke to my spirit, drowning out the music and singing all around me. The great I AM was speaking.

Figuratively, Jesus pointed at me and motioned me forward. I was drawn to the altar, to my knees, into confession, and to His Lordship.

I surrendered my life to Jesus that day. I like to say, "Years before it became a point and click world, Jesus pointed, everything clicked, and my life was forever changed."

Who cared that I was a skinny little girl who didn't know much about anything? Who cared if I was the last one chosen by team captains on the playground? He, the Lord, had redeemed me. He'd summoned me by name.

I left church that day in love with the Lord and eager to tell someone, anyone, everyone. Years later, I am still that girl who took the unseen hand of the Lord that day to begin a lifelong pursuit of walking by faith.

Through the years, as I've experienced many of life's ups and downs, I've found that God is faithful. When we grasp His unseen hand and follow him through the shadows of life He will show us great and marvelous things.

Will you take time today to dedicate yourself before the Lord that He might do mighty, great, amazing, and marvelous things in and through you?

*Let us hold unswervingly to the hope we profess,
for he who promised is faithful.*
Hebrews 10:23

Prayer

Sweet Jesus, thank You for reaching out to me with mercy and grace. I invite You to take hold of me and to hold me close this day as I take hold of You. Give me the determination to hold unswervingly to You for You are my hope and my Lord.

Tuesday
A Psalm for Life

The LORD is my Shepherd.
Psalm 23:1

I was first exposed to Psalm 23 when I was in elementary school. One of my favorite grade-school teachers, Mrs. Collins, began each day with Scripture reading and prayer, a pattern formed in my life then that I have carried into adulthood. She introduced me to Psalm 23 and proceeded to lead everyone in the class to memorize the entire chapter. I didn't know at the time that would be one of the most life-altering school activities I'd ever done.

Through high school and college I learned many things from writing geometric proofs to writing grant proposals. What I turn to in times of need, however, is the Word of God. Psalm 23 has been a staple, helping me to cope through both sleepless nights and demanding days.

I've repeated those verses more times than I can count. When my husband, Don, was laid off from his job the Lord was our good Shepherd, our faithful and proven provider, able to meet our physical, emotional, and spiritual needs. In that time of uncertainty, He unfailingly offered us security, peace, and soul restoration.

At other times when we sought direction concerning relocation, a major purchase, or other important choices, we looked to the Lord. He was there to lead and guide us just as promised.

The words of that simple Psalm have encouraged me when I was lonely, afraid, or feeling insignificant. The truths of the chapter have carried me through childhood wants and grown-up worries. When I have experienced serious loss, I've found in it comfort, hope, and assurance. Unpleasant circumstances are palatable in light of the promise that Jesus is with me through it all.

When one of my good friends was dying of cancer, she was entering the unknown, a place of fear, except for the fact that Jesus was with her. When she expelled her last breath, she went home with her Lord to live with Him forever. I learned at her bedside that passing from death into eternal life is peaceful. He who is peace walked with her through the valley of death and into eternity.

He was there, even in the shadow of death, and she is now dwelling forever in the house of the Lord. I look forward to the day when I will see my dear friend again. Until then I am convinced that goodness and mercy will follow me all the days of my life and I, too, will dwell with the Lord forever.

Want to do something to enhance your view of the Lordship of Jesus? Begin today by committing Psalm 23 to memory. You'll be glad you did.

The Lord is my shepherd, I shall not be in want.
He makes me lie down in green pastures,
he leads me beside quiet waters,
he restores my soul.
He guides me in paths of righteousness
for his name's sake.
Even though I walk
through the valley of the shadow of death,
I will fear no evil,
for you are with me;
your rod and your staff,

they comfort me.
You prepare a table before me
in the presence of my enemies.
You anoint my head with oil;
my cup overflows.
Surely goodness and love will follow me
all the days of my life,
and I will dwell in the house of the Lord
forever.

Prayer

Lord, You are truly the Good Shepherd. We invite You to be Lord of this day and of all the days of our lives. Thank You for Your gracious love and provision. Most of all, thank You that You are with us always even in the valley of the shadow of death. Give us courage to face the day ahead and all the days of our lives with the assurance that we will someday live with You forever.

Wednesday
Plunged into Darkness

Weeping may remain for a night
but rejoicing comes in the morning.
Psalm 30:5b

I well remember the night after my initial diagnosis of retina disease. I lay awake, eyes wide open, "trying on" the pitch black of blindness. Darkness engulfed me, both inside and out. My bed was a dark pit that threatened to swallow me whole. Though my vision hadn't changed that day I was plunged into emotional darkness, an abyss of questions. I'd encountered the black hole of fear and fallen into it.

Let's face it. The absence of light is scary. Not only does it limit our ability to see, it also carries an implication of evil. Simple sounds become whispers of doom. Shadowy shapes are creatures that threaten. If given a choice, anyone would choose light, choose sight.

I remembered a friend who worked with a blind man. She loved to tell about the time she got to the office late and found her co-worker sitting in the pitch dark. He was working away as usual. "Why didn't you turn on the lights?" she complained to him. "You scared me half to death! Didn't you realize I could have tripped over the furniture or bumped into the wall?" She went on with her rant until she came to her senses. Silence filled the room until the good-natured man laughingly replied, "Welcome to my world, hon. Welcome to my world." What had been a nuisance to my friend was her co-worker's reality—always night, never day.

Still lying in the dark, I wished I could laugh about darkness as freely as that man had and display his joy that defied blindness. Though he lived in a physically darkened world, he laughed easily. Not me. The mere suggestion that I would be blind left me sad and scared. I swiped at the tears rolling toward my ears as unanswered questions pulled me lower. What was I to do? How would I cope? When my vision failed, how could I be a good wife and mother?

Question marks continued to punctuate my mind and fill the air until I finally fell asleep. When morning came, I opened my eyes. Whew! I could still see. Rays of sunshine streaming through the blinds had swallowed the darkness. What a relief. Seeing the light of day excited me.

I couldn't think how long it had been since a sunrise had so captured my attention. Light spilled warmth and spoke hope and courage to me. The potential of the new day brought with it a fresh outlook. I thanked God for the gift of another morning and for the blessing of eyesight. I realized that until that morning I'd taken the gift of seeing every day of my life for granted.

The rising sun reminded me the Lord was still on the throne. The news of RP had taken *me* by surprise, but not *God*. He was well-aware of me. I took comfort in knowing He was still in complete control. The sun had come up that day just like always and I clearly saw in it the faithfulness of God.

The same God who in the beginning spoke light into darkness still speaks light into darkness today. We can rejoice always and every day in the Lord for He surely does great things. Only He can turn our sorrows into joy.

Having a hard day today? In a season of sadness? If so, hold onto your faith and hold out for renewed rejoicing. Say with the Psalmist, "Weeping may remain for a night, but rejoicing comes in the morning" (Psalm 30:5b).

Prayer

Lord, we cry out to You from the darkness that threatens to cover us. We ask You to speak light into the dark areas of our lives, into those areas where we need the light of Your presence and the light of Your word. We acknowledge Jesus as the Light of the World and ask that His light would brighten our worlds today. Pull us up, Lord. Wipe our tears and remind us that weeping lasts only until joy breaks forth in the morning light.

Thursday
Looking Up

I lift up my eyes to the hills—
where does my help come from?
My help comes from the Lord,
the Maker of heaven and earth.
Psalm 121:1-2

Joe was a man who knew a thing or two about suffering. He was young when his mother died. Though left in the care of his grieving father, he felt alone. His jealous older brothers hated him so much they couldn't say one kind word to him.

Eventually, Joe's brothers threw him into an empty well. Later, they faked his death and sold him as a slave to foreigners. In the new country, with its strange culture, he was put to work. He won the respect of others and His life circumstances were improving—until his boss's wife made a pass at him. When Joe refused her advances, she got angry. Then she got even. She falsely accused him of sexual assault. As a result, he lost his position and was thrown in jail.

Joe sounds like a character from a modern-day movie, but he isn't. He's actually from the Bible (Genesis 37, 39-42).

Joseph knew what it was like to be thrown into a deep dark hole and left for dead. While he'd never been told he would be blind, like me, he was familiar with pits of other kinds, underground dungeons where he called out to hear only his own voice echo back. He was hurled into darkness time and again. His life, like ours, was filled with plans gone awry, dreams turned to nightmares. Yet when we read Joseph's story we see that he somehow avoided the perpetual pity-party mindset we often adopt. No "I'm trapped in the storm drain of life" talk, either.

The key to Joseph's survival was in the focus of his gaze. When he was in the pit he avoided looking at the imprisoning walls, the cold hard ground, or the impossible climb. Instead, he looked up. Eyes heavenward, he gazed into the light and God illumined the dark places. He lifted Joseph out of the pit, freed him from bondage, and released him from prison.

I would imagine most of us have been in a pit of some sort—possibly right this minute. If you aren't in one now you may be about to fall into one or dusting yourself off after just climbing out of one. Whatever the case, remember Jesus' words: "I have told you these things so that in me you may have peace. In this world, you will have trouble. But take heart! I have overcome the world" (John 16:33).

In other words, trouble is a given. Situational pits are part of life. The good news is Jesus overcame so we can overcome. Whatever your pit, be encouraged. Take heart. Be of good cheer. And let the light of God's presence brighten the way.

Prayer

Dear Maker of heaven and earth,
I lift my eyes to You this day. Would You open my eyes to see beyond my problems to the help found in You? When I fall into situational pits, remind me that Jesus has overcome so I can, too.
I love You, Lord, and thank You for loving me.

Friday
Bifocals

Forget the former things;
do not dwell on the past.
See, I am doing a new thing!
Now it springs up; do you not perceive it?
I am making a way in the desert
and streams in the wasteland.
Isaiah 43:18-19

Most of us are creatures of habit, aren't we? We often want to hold onto what is comfortable and familiar. The unexpected makes us nervous and change doesn't come easily.

A friend of ours jokes about the day he learned his wife was pregnant with their third child. He says, "I thought our family was complete, but God apparently had another idea." Middle-aged and slightly balding, the concept came as quite a shock. "You know you're in trouble," he laughed, "when you have to pull out your bifocals to read the pregnancy test."

With the news of the family expansion came visions of change—diapers, routines, and schedules, just to name a few things. He laughingly claims that being a new father later in life changed his prayer life, too. "Mostly, I ask God to let this child get out of diapers before I have to be in them and to let him get on solid foods before I have to start gumming mine."

Change is hard. Yet it is necessary for spiritual growth. If we always do what we've always done we'll always be what we've always been. Jesus Himself experienced the agony of change. When He was born, He became a human.

He transitioned from deity to diapers. He was God wrapped in swaddling clothes and laid in a manger.

He grew into a man called into a new vocation. I imagine He had been quite at home working in Joseph's carpenter's shop. When the time came, however, for Him to lay down the tool belt and take up the cross, Jesus did it. He left His home and what was familiar to set out for the unknown. God was doing a new thing in His life and there was no time to waste dwelling on the past.

When my vision began to change for the worse, I wasn't excited about the future. The new thing God was doing in my life was painful. Instead of going where I wanted when I wanted, I had to depend on others to take me wherever I went. After years of practically living out of my car, I couldn't even make it alone to the end of our street and back. I missed the enjoyment of driving. I also missed the freedom and independence of walking by myself through the mall, at the park, and other places. Travelling by sighted guide had its own pride issues. I feared that I appeared mentally deficient as well as visually impaired. I was thankful for and appreciated the help, yet I hated feeling like a bother. I didn't want to be a burden.

With each drop in my vision I ached for the past and dreaded the future. When I eventually lost the ability to read printed materials I felt like I'd lost a friend. I liked the feel of magazines and books. I enjoyed the smoothness of the glossy pages and the sturdy compactness of the bindings. The same was true with my Bible. I loved flipping through the thin pages to read highlighted or underlined passages. I didn't want to listen to it on my iPod. I wanted to hold it in my hands.

I resisted the changes in my vision and the resulting changes in my life. I wished I could hold onto the past, to do things I'd always done, to be what I'd always been.

Over time, I adjusted to my new normal. As I spent time listening to my Bible and praying I stopped wishing things were different. God seemed to take away the wishbone in me and replace it with a little backbone. When I finally began to let go of the comforts I had been clinging to so tightly God began to reveal new things He wanted to do in me. Vision loss became the catalyst for greater things God had in mind, changing me from the inside out.

I soon discovered that faith really does come by "hearing" the word. Scripture passages I'd highlighted came to life in new ways as I listened to them. One treasured verse that helped me navigate the dark valley of visual impairment was Romans 8:28: "In all things God works for the good of those who love Him, who have been called according to His purpose" (Romans 8:28).

Regardless of how my vision changes, I know God is at work. And He is working *for* me, not *against* me. Though I'm a doubter at times, the sentiment in one of my favorite songs really is true. During the times when I can't "trace God's hand" I can most definitely "trust His heart."

So can you. Whatever the changes in this season of your life, rest assured, dear one, that God is doing a new thing. Do you sense it? It is springing up even now. Do you believe me? If not, pull out your bifocals and see for yourself. The test result is in and it is positive. God is birthing something new in and through you. Get ready. Change is on the way.

Prayer

Thank You, Lord, that You are always up to new things in our lives. Increase our perception and turn our attention to the fresh work You desire. When we are tempted to look over our shoulders and cling to the past lead us to anticipate Your will and plan. Help us to keep our eyes forward and on You. When changes occur in our lives, fill us with an expectation that You are birthing something that will ultimately draw us closer to You. Increase our faith that You are always working for us and never against us.

Weekend Reflections

Saturday-Sunday

Grasping the Unseen Hand

Grab your Bible, a notebook, and a pen, and let's withdraw to a quiet place for time with the Lord.

Are you exhausted, frustrated, and ready to give up? If so, let your breaking point become a turning point. Turn it all over to the Lord.

Read Matthew 6:25-34

- List the cares and concerns on your heart today.
- Give those cares and concerns to Jesus.
- Memorize verse 26:

  Look at the birds of the air; they do not sow or reap or store away in barns, and yet your heavenly Father feeds them. Are you not much more valuable than they?

Write out your reflections from today's time with the Lord.

Prayer

Thank You, Lord, that I am more valuable to You than the birds of the air. I trust You with everything that concerns me.

Week Two

Monday
Take Time to Slow Down

Do nothing out of selfish ambition or vain conceit,
but in humility consider others
better than yourselves.
Each of you should look not only
to your own interests,
but also to the interests of others.
Philippians 2:3-4

I paced the floor, stopping occasionally to check my watch and sigh loudly. Tapping my foot, I looked up to the heavens and waved my arms as if that might make things better. Every few minutes I walked back to the bedroom where Don was still sleeping. I didn't want to wake him; I just wanted him to wake up. "Why can't he be more like me?" I asked myself. Didn't he know we needed to hurry? Hadn't I mentioned that I wanted to get an early start to the day? Didn't he care?

With every minute that passed my stomach churned, turned, and burned a little more. I felt further and further behind, though the only deadline was the one in my mind. I'd mapped out a schedule and I wanted to stick to it. As usual, I was high strung, tightly wound, and ticking fast.

My type-A inner voice was getting more and more insistent. After all, was it too much to ask that we keep to the routine? Hadn't I managed Saturday mornings well in the past? Wasn't that how we got everything accomplished that needed to be done? My blood pressure was rising and I was moving quickly from frustrated to angry.

I liked setting the alarm and heading out early with my "to go, to do, to buy" lists in hand. Every Saturday I was on the prowl, a huntress eager for conquests.

Patience and waiting were not my strong suits, so since I'd had to stop driving I was often a nervous wreck. Don was usually my chauffeur and I was forced to synchronize my schedule to his—not as simple as it sounds.

When it came to managing Saturday mornings, we operated in opposite time warps. Don liked sleeping in and relaxing into the day. His internal body clock was set on "slow and steady." He often joked that he is so laid back his pulse has to be taken using a calendar instead of a second hand. Even my grandmother, in her eighties at the time, observed, "Don, you're not so fast-moving are you?" That said it all.

So with Don as my primary driver, I had to adjust my body clock to "Don-speed." It didn't matter how early I got up and got ready. To Don, "up and out" meant hitting the driveway at the crack of noon. By that time I usually felt "left behind" as I imagined other shoppers getting the best parking spaces and finding the best deals. I missed driving myself around town, checking items off my list, and arriving back home with a trunk stuffed with groceries and a backseat strewn with dry cleaning and shopping bags.

For many weeks, that Saturday scene repeated itself. I was uptight and unhappy. I wanted to do things my own way. As weeks passed, though, I sensed a few attitude adjustments taking shape. I noticed change—not in Don, as I'd first hoped—in me. The Lord had been dealing with my selfishness as He reminded me that Don was a hard-working person who deserved the chance to ease into his weekend. So what if I couldn't go where I wanted to go on my own timetable? The greater blessing was in the fact that I had a caring and good-natured husband who was willing to drive me at all.

During those Saturday morning waits God reminded me that I should always be "...quick to listen, slow to speak and slow to become angry, for man's anger does not bring about the righteous life that God desires" (James 1:19b-20). My frustration and impatience were not pleasing to God.

I wanted to change. But in order to do that I had to yield the driver's seat of my life to God. Instead of demanding my own way, I needed to not only look to my own interests, "but also to the interests of others" (Philippians 2:4b).

Who's in your driver's seat? Why not take this opportunity to consider your own attitudes? Are there any that could use adjusting? Do you, like me, tend to be occasionally self-focused and self-centered? There is hope! We have a Gentle Shepherd who lovingly reminds us of the needs and desires of those around us. If we accept His guidance not only will we be less stressed, we will, as Paul promised the Philippians, "shine like stars in the universe" (Philippians 2: 15).

Prayer

Father, examine our hearts today.
Show us if there are attitudes that need adjusting. Begin any corrective work that needs to be done in our hearts, souls, and minds. Give us the wisdom to be slow to speak, quick to listen, and slow to become angry. Transform us into the likeness of Christ who always treated others as better than Himself. Lord, forgive us when we fail and pick us up when we fall.
Then strengthen us to try again.

Tuesday
Follow Only Him

Since we live by the Spirit,
let us keep in step with the Spirit.
Galatians 5:25

Being led by the Spirit—keeping in step with Him—is similar to traveling by sighted guide. After losing much of my central and peripheral vision, I have become unable to walk in unfamiliar settings without assistance. I need mobility help. So I have had to learn how to travel with a sighted guide. In order to move successfully from one place to another, I have to take the arm of the other person and then rely on them completely for directional cues. If I'm going to follow their lead and keep in step with their stride I have to concentrate totally on what they are saying and doing.

In our spiritual walk, the Holy Spirit, through the Word of God, acts as our sighted guide. If we are to walk successfully in the Spirit we have to follow His lead and listen to His words. Once we accept the fact that we are in need of a Spiritual Sighted Guide, taking the Spirit's arm and trusting Him to lead us in accordance with the written Word comes naturally. The Spirit is reliable. He will never lead us astray. He will always speak what is in agreement with God's ways as recorded in the Bible.

Traveling by sighted guide has taught me that we have two ears and one mouth for a very practical reason. If I'm talking when I should be listening I can get into big trouble. I'm thinking God probably intends that we spend twice as much time listening to Him as talking to Him.

One night when Don and I were out together, I asked him to guide me to the ladies room. As we walked, I was talking excitedly. I felt Don's footsteps pause, but I kept right on talking and stepped beyond him. I couldn't figure out why he kept trying to interrupt me. A few steps into the bathroom, I understood. The cold fixture hanging from the wall said it all. To my horror and Don's delight, I was in the men's room.

Walking with a sighted guide is a learning process. So is walking in the Spirit and keeping in step with Him. Both require practice. Let's face it. Relying on someone else's vision instead of our own is not easy. We want to be independent, to go our own way and do our own thing. Instead of taking the arm of the Spirit and walking slightly behind Him, we ignore the offer of His guiding elbow and rush ahead of Him. We refuse His advice to stop, wait, and beware. We run headlong into dangerous situations. In spite of limited vision and limited knowledge we insist on going our own way.

Given my present sightlessness, I would physically stumble or trip and fall if I struck out without the help of someone who sees. The same is true for each of us in the spiritual realm. When we set out headlong ahead of the Holy Spirit we are bound to figuratively trip or stumble and fall.

Are you headed out on your own and in the wrong direction? Why not pause right where you are and listen for the Lord? Ask Him to open your eyes to see and your ears to hear Him. Invite Him to take the lead as you commit to always and only follow Him.

Prayer

Holy Lord, would You open my eyes to see You today? Would You open my ears that I might hear and follow Your voice? I release control of my life to You. Forgive me for the times and ways I've struck out on my own when You were extending Your guiding elbow. I submit to Your leadership and commit to always and only follow You.

Wednesday
Out of the Wreckage

The thief comes only to steal and kill and destroy;
I have come that they may have life,
and have it to the full.
John 10:10

One of the Christmas seasons after I learned I had retinitis pigmentosa was the craziest time of my life. I think I was subconsciously trying to compensate for any future limits I would experience. If I wasn't always going to be able to drive, I would certainly get a lifetime of driving in before my vision failed!

I was a perpetual juggler, tossing one spinning plate in the air after another. I had three young children, all boys, all active in sports and other activities. My husband and I taught Bible study classes. We sang in the choir, served on committees, and led other ministries. In addition, I helped my mother care for my grandmother. I volunteered at the school and worked part-time. Everything I was involved in was good, but all of it took time. Most days were hectic multiplied by two. In the hoopla, my housework was often neglected.

I remember one morning in particular. It was the last day of school for the boys before Christmas break. I had homemade goodies to take to school. I had teachers' gifts to wrap and three boys' heads to comb and push out the door. My house was already a mess. Bible costumes lined the sofa in the TV room waiting to be washed and pressed for a big production. Dishes stood in the kitchen sink, on the counter, on the table, and wherever else they could be stacked. Garlands and lights lay at the base of the stairs waiting to be hung. Boxes of Christmas decorations cluttered the living room. I pulled out the teachers' gifts to wrap at the last minute, adding tape, scissors, shopping bags, and wrapping paper to the mix. After I tied the last bow and sent the boys to the van with the packages, I yanked curly ribbon off my shoe and pulled the front door shut behind me.

As I backed the van out of the driveway I remember thinking, if an inspector from the health department stopped by today I'd be in big trouble. He'd hang a "condemned" sign right across the front door. Looking back at the house, I silently prayed, "Lord, please just let me get home before someone sends out a wrecking ball."

Then I did what any good mother would do. I plastered my best room-mom smile on my face and headed into the school. My plan was to straighten and clean the minute I arrived home later in the day. I didn't know I would be coming home that afternoon to a "Come to Jesus" meeting.

I spent a few hours at the school then pulled back into our driveway. I was surprised to see an unfamiliar car there. It was empty. I wondered where the driver might be. That's when I noticed the front door of my house standing open. Okay, the door is open and there's a strange car in the driveway. I was a little afraid I might find a robber inside. Should I go in or run? Then I reasoned that a thief would be more deceptive than to park his car in front of the house and leave the door open. So cautiously, I moved forward, up the steps, and through the front door. I looked around. There standing in the middle of the mess was not a *robber* as I had feared, but a *Robert*. Robert Jones, to be exact.

Robert Jones was a young man my husband and I had taught in the youth group when he was a teenager. He'd visited our home many times before. This, however, was the first time he'd seen it in such a state of horrible disarray. Robert stood in the living room, phone in hand, ready to call 911. He thought my house had been ransacked and I had been kidnapped.

I was mortified. In the haste of the morning, I'd apparently failed to pull the door completely closed. When Robert had knocked on the door it had swung open. And the house was in such a state of chaos Robert thought a thief had ravaged the place.

As I stood there in the middle of the wreckage I realized what I saw physically represented what was going on with me spiritually. The scene screamed disheveled disorder. I came to terms with the truth: "My life is a mess, too. My life is—a—mess."

I scanned the room again and wanted to cry. This was my "Come to Jesus" moment, an epiphany. I fully grasped and was saddened to admit that my spiritual house was a wreck, as well. While I'd been busy going to church and participating in every ministry possible, I'd neglected my relationship with God. Somewhere in all the "busy-ness," time spent alone with Jesus had gone right out of my day.

Beth Moore says, "If Satan can't make you bad, he'll make you busy." That's what was happening in my life. I was a good person doing good things, but I was neglecting reading the Bible consistently and praying regularly. In my "Come to Jesus" moment, words I'd read in the Bible rushed back to me. "Come to me, all you who are weary and burdened, and I will give you rest" (Matthew 11:28-29).

I was shocked and relieved that the God of the universe, the Maker of Heaven and Earth, didn't wait for me to clean the house before He showed up. With dishes stacked in the sink and wrinkled Bible costumes lying around, He came and offered me rest. He didn't yell at me for being a slob or scold me for neglecting Him. Instead, He whispered sweetly, "I see you. The load you're carrying is heavy. Would you put it down for a minute? Here, come sit with me. Rest."

In that moment, I became well aware of the true "robber" that had been at work. The Bible says the thief comes to steal, to kill, and to destroy. I was a spiritual wreck because I'd let the enemy set my schedule. I'd allowed him to steal my quiet time, kill my consistent Bible reading, and destroy my personal prayer life. I'd forfeited developing my relationship with God for church work.

A friend of mine says, "If you're too busy for God, you're too busy." I was in constant motion until Jesus invited me to come to Him, to find my rest in Him.

So, let me ask you a question. Is there a robber in your spiritual house? Is he stealing your quiet time, killing your consistent Bible reading, and destroying your personal prayer life? If so, resist him and he will flee from you. Draw near to God and He will draw near to you (James 4:7-8).

Prayer

Thank You, loving Father, for meeting us right where we are and for issuing an invitation to us to find our rest in You. Forgive us when we neglect our relationship to You by neglecting Bible reading and prayer. Show us any areas of disarray as You faithfully clean our spiritual houses. We invite
You to come into the messes of our lives to pull us out of the wreckage and into Your waiting arms.

Thursday
Are You a Shoe-Booty?

Jesus replied, "No one who puts his hand to the plow and looks back is fit for service in the kingdom of God."
Luke 9:62

Though I've, on occasion, mistakenly worn one black shoe with one brown shoe, I've never been forced by necessity to wear a mismatched pair. Quite the contrary, actually. I am extremely shoe-blessed.

Not so with Archie Bunker of the famed and often irreverent old situation comedy, *All in the Family*. While I don't claim to agree with Archie Bunker on any subject, I do remember one episode when he shared a heart-wrenching story from his fictitious childhood.

When Archie was a boy, his family was too poor to buy him a new pair of shoes, so he wore what he had. Every morning he pulled on one sneaker and one boot. Naturally, kids in the neighborhood began to taunt him. As he walked to school, they chanted, "Rooty, tooty, here comes Shoe-Booty."

Sad story for a sitcom, huh? It's really a tear-jerker, though, when the scenario is real and believers live like Shoe-Booties. We do that when we humbly wear prayer, Bible reading, church attendance, and other Godly pursuits on one foot while the other foot boasts materialism, pride, selfish ambition, and idolatry. With one foot dressed for God and the other for the world, we are spiritual Shoe-Booties.

The Bible, in James 4, cautions against such fickleness. Believers are advised to pursue total commitment. The writer's message is passionate and straightforward. He warns that flirting with the world is nothing short of spiritual infidelity. "You adulterous people, don't you know that friendship with the world is hatred toward God? Anyone who chooses to be a friend of the world becomes an enemy of God. Or do you think Scripture says without reason that the spirit he caused to live in us envies intensely?" (James 4:4-5).

James correctly compares friendship with the world to an illicit affair where the unfaithful Christian breaks his/her marriage vow to God. He asserts that compatibility with the world and harmony with the Holy Spirit is impossible. The Spirit of God in us pines for our unadulterated affection and seeks our undying love. He desires our complete devotion to Him. And undefiled and undivided love for Him is best for us as well.

God designed us in such a way that we are most content when we are led by the Spirit and when we keep in step with Him. The world's ways may seem appetizing and fulfilling, but don't be fooled. Pursuing worldliness will leave you with a bitter taste in your mouth and emptiness in your soul. It's no wonder the Bible tells us to choose to be either spiritually hot or cold. God is sickened by lukewarm believers. They are half-hearted, double-minded Shoe-Booties.

Are you conflicted choosing between God's ways and the ways of the world? How would you classify yourself spiritually? Are you hot, cold, or lukewarm? Maybe it's time to take a look at your spiritual footwear. Are they mismatched? Is one of your shoes decorated with crosses and fish symbols while the other is covered with dollar signs and status symbols? If so, you are in need of a Designer shoe makeover. Let the very one who designed you fit you with the right footwear and the right size. Follow Paul's fashion advice. In Ephesians, he tells us to fit our feet "with the readiness that comes from the gospel of peace" (Ephesians 6:15). That is one wardrobe essential our heavenly Designer intended.

If you're trying to serve both God and the world, it'll never work. Wearing one shoe and one boot will get you nowhere. Serving two lords is impossible. The Bible says, "No one can serve two masters. Either he will hate the one and love the other, or he will be devoted to the one and despise the other" (Matthew 6:24).

Instead of Shoe-Booties, fill your spiritual closet with good things—God things—for the best look ever. Pair the Spirit of God with the Word of God for a perfect pair and perfect fit. Together, the two will enhance your spiritual walk and you'll enjoy the adventure of being led by the Spirit and keeping in step with Him.

Prayer

Father God, today we simply ask You to give us an undivided heart of love for You as we seek to walk by the Spirit and keep in step with Him.

Friday
Stop Circling the Perimeter

Whether you turn to the right or the left,
your ears will hear a voice behind you, saying,
"This is the way; walk in it."
Isaiah 30:21

Traffic snarls, delays, and jams are a nuisance, aren't they? They slow us down and we don't like to brake for anything. We are a people in a hurry. We don't have any extra minutes to waste sitting in traffic. In this age of Google Maps and GPS devices we check traffic reports, traffic conditions, and traffic alerts trying to scoot around—what else?—traffic. All these advances in technology have made navigating in metro areas easier. If you don't believe me, just ask Pascual Perez who learned the importance of maps the hard way.

Perez was a young pitcher called up from the Atlanta Braves' Richmond farm team in 1982. He was first introduced to driving in metro Atlanta on the same day he was scheduled to throw his first pitch in a Braves uniform. He'd made it to the big leagues. It was an exciting time for Braves fans, whose beloved team was in a pennant race. Everyone looked forward to the debut of the up-and-coming hopeful, Pascual Perez. Perez was supposed to arrive in town that Saturday and take his place on the mound as the starting pitcher. He was to toss the first ball at 7:05pm.

When it came time for the game to start, however, Perez was nowhere to be found. That's because he was not in the stadium—he was circling it. In fact, he was driving his rental car around and around the city trying to locate the field. He looped the 65-mile I-285 Atlanta perimeter highway three times before running out of gas. When he finally got to the game, frenzied by his ordeal and tangled in chaos, he'd missed the first few innings and ended up sitting on the bench. Instead of being known as a player that rounded the bases, he is remembered for rounding the perimeter. As a result, he was tagged with the nickname *Perimeter Perez.*

Through circumstances, sometimes beyond our control, chaos creeps into our lives, throwing a wrench into our schedules and playing havoc with our time. Have you had news that sent you mentally circling the perimeter, seeking a way to navigate uncharted territory? What unexpected event has sent you reeling or left you feeling lost? Maybe you learned a loved one has terminal cancer. Perhaps an MRI report revealed that your child has a tumor and needed surgery. You may be struggling to parent your children. Or, like me, maybe you went for a routine eye exam and were told you had an eye disease and would someday be blind.

Whatever your circumstances, calm in the middle of chaos is possible. We're always going to be busy and life will always throw us curve balls like it did for Perimeter Perez. We're going to find ourselves circling the perimeter, uncertain where we're going, unless we spend time with God on a regular basis, daily coming to Him who joyfully bears our burdens.

Do you need a little calm in the middle of an otherwise chaotic existence? Do you feel lost in confusion, circling the perimeter of God's will, but never reaching the destination He has planned for you? If so, pull out the most reliable road map of all, your Bible. Position yourself in the presence of the Lord. Then listen for that still small voice as He whispers, "This is the way; walk in it" (Isaiah 30:21).

Prayer

Precious Lord and Faithful Guide,
would You show us the way to Your plan for
our lives? Would You speak to us from Your Word and
whisper to us in our spirits? In times of chaos and
confusion, quiet us in Your presence and
clarify which direction we should go. Let us take Your
counsel and operate in the center of Your will.

Weekend Reflections
Saturday-Sunday

Grasping the Unseen Hand

Grab your Bible, a notebook, and a pen, and let's withdraw to a quiet place for time with the Lord.

Are you in a mess of your own making? Have you made some mistakes you now regret? If so, be encouraged with what God can do.

God can make all things new.

> *He can take the madness that surrounds you*
> *and weave meaning into it.*
> *He can take the mess you've made of things*
> *and give you a message.*
> *He can take the mistakes you regret*
> *and use you on His mission field.*

Read Acts 22:4-16.

Memorize 2 Corinthians 5:17:

> *Therefore, if anyone is in Christ, he is a new creation; the old has gone, the new has come!*

Write out your reflections from today's time with the Lord.

Prayer

Thank You, Lord, that You make all things new.

Week Three

Monday
His Grace Still Amazes Me

Everyone born of God overcomes the world.
This is the victory that has overcome the world, even our faith.
1 John 5:4

My grandpa has always been my hero. He was special. One eye had been injured in a farming accident and over time he lost sight in the other as well. Though he couldn't see, I never thought of him as blind. Instead, I remember him being filled with light and laughter. His Godliness—and a good laugh—drew people to him like lemonade on a hot day.

Grandpa lived with my grandmother in a beautiful old farmhouse. In summer, a tree whose branches sagged with ripening pears anchored the front yard. Wooden rocking chairs lined the front porch, and the kitchen smelled of sweet fried pies and pickled cucumbers. In the back, sunshine filtering through the leaves of an old oak produced playful patterns of light on the ground. Neighbors, friends, and relatives often gathered there, sitting in cane-bottomed chairs, deep in conversation. Their words floated through the screened doors into the cool interior of the house.

My grandfather offered up heaping helpings of God in his lighthearted way. He'd kept his faith and his sense of humor in spite of blindness. I want to do the same.

I wonder, will my grandchildren someday play the same jokes on me that my twin brother and I played on our grandfather? When we were five or six years old we loved to good-naturedly trick him. We'd welcome him into our house with open arms and happy hearts. The minute he'd walk in the front door, we'd verbally direct him to a "comfortable" chair. We'd excitedly chime, "Here, Grandpa, this way. Over here. A little further. Okay, Grandpa, you can sit down now."

With a broad, knowing smile he'd ask, "Here? Is the chair right behind me?"

"Yes, Grandpa," we'd giggle. "Go ahead. Sit down."

Inevitably, he'd lean backward and plop on the floor just as we'd planned and we'd all collapse in laughter. I can't remember when we first started playing that game. I now understand that Grandpa knew all along what we were up to. He indulged our young hearts with twinkling blue eyes and easy laughter. He saw to it we had fun. His rich faith in the Lord allowed him to enjoy the funnier side of blindness. He didn't let vision loss dampen his spirit. He managed to trust God while looking at the lighter side of life.

With his focus on God, my grandfather kept his faith in spite of difficulty. As a result, he was able to do more than survive. Though tossed in the deep well of sightlessness, enslaved to the burden of blindness, and confined to a dungeon of darkness, he overcame. And he thrived.

During the last months of his life, my grandpa was confined to a hospital bed. There he continued to bear witness to the Lord, especially in song. *Amazing Grace* was his favorite. He sang it often and without hesitation. When he sang, "I once was lost but now I'm found, was blind but now I see," he made a believer out of me. I understood the truth of what my grandpa was singing. He saw some things none of us could see as his faith was being made sight.

The grace my grandpa sung of truly is amazing. "For it is by grace you have been saved through faith—and this not from yourselves, it is the gift of God" (Ephesians 2:8).

Thank God today for His amazing grace.

Prayer

Sweet Jesus, thank You for Your amazing, saving grace. Thank You for giving grace that is sufficient for us no matter what comes our way. Thank You, Lord, that it is by grace we are redeemed through belief. Thank You for the gift of grace. And thank You that after all these years Your grace is high enough, wide enough, and incredible enough to still be amazing. How sweet, so sweet, is the grace You offer. Thank You, Lord, for holding us in the grip of grace as we, by grace, hold to Your unseen hand.

Tuesday
Stormy Weather

Consider it pure joy, my brothers,
whenever you face trials of many kinds,
because you know that the testing of your faith develops perseverance. Perseverance must finish its work so that you may be mature and complete,
not lacking anything.
James 1:2-3

Aren't those ideal moments great when the job is fulfilling, the marriage is perfect, the kids are angelic, the bills are paid, and the skies are clear? This Utopian state, however, rarely exists except in fairy tales and dreams. Reality is not that smooth. The truth is most of us fall into one of three categories. We're either in the middle of a storm, heading into one, or coming out of one.

Storms are a given. So what are we to do about it? When Doppler radar reflects a tornado on the ground headed toward us, most of us move quickly to the safest place we can find. In the same way, when adversities—teenage rebellion, parental illness, workplace downsizing, and the like—take us by storm we have to be ready to take appropriate action. But how?

Daily we are bombarded with choice-points, times when we have to choose how to respond to difficult situations. Will we trust God when His way is not the most convenient or pleasant? When our beliefs are tested, will we stand firmly on God's word or will we stumble and fall?

Trials that test our faith come in various forms. Blood-work reveals an incurable disease. A promotion requires a cross-country move. Your child is a prisoner of addiction. You are forced to either go forward with God or try to maintain the status quo. Following God is the right thing to do, but you wonder how you can trust Him in the throes of such uncertainty. All your life you've had your ladder leaning against the Lord and you suddenly fear the next rung. The disease may be too painful, the move too demanding, the addiction too binding. And so you frantically seek to muster at least the faith of a mustard seed.

In times of discomfort we can take comfort in knowing that God is using the hard times to perfect us. We are, in fact, told to be joyful when we meet trials. I don't know about you, but joy isn't usually my first reaction when trouble comes. My inclinations are more along the lines of shrinking back, hiding under the bed, and eating lots of chocolate.

Scripture, however, teaches that every trial has its own purpose. Nothing comes to us without first being sifted through the fingers of God. And James assures us that the end result of joyfully persevering in times of testing is spiritual maturity.

Are you under the gun right now? Staring down the barrel of trials of many kinds? If so, you are in excellent company—Jesus' company, in fact. Scripture reminds us that He endured the cross, ignoring unimaginable pain and shame, for the joy set before Him. Then he encouraged us to do the same.

So hang in there. Stormy weather is sure to come, but there could be no flowers without it.

Prayer

Heavenly Father, show us how to view life through the lens of joy. When storms form on the horizon, give us the faith to trust You. Enable us to persevere through every hardship and trial for the joy of the maturity that will follow. Just as Jesus endured the cross for the joy set before Him, so let us endure for the sake of the joys to come.

Wednesday
Power Up to Overcome

In all these things we are more than conquerors through Him who loves us.
Romans 8:37

Since she was one of my mentors, I considered my outings with my friend Janice educational experiences. Although in constant pain from rheumatoid arthritis, she was an incredible Bible teacher and prayer warrior. She taught me how to find meaning in life—and some really good deals on purses.

Interesting things always happened when Janice and I hit the mall. When they saw us coming, shoppers parted like the Red Sea. With her toodling around in her power chair and me tapping my white cane alongside her, they had no choice.

We were an odd sight. I don't think people knew quite how to handle us. I imagine they focused on our inabilities. They didn't realize the only limits that really mattered at the mall were our credit limits. Otherwise we were pretty unflappable, Janice even more so than me.

Keeping up with Janice had always been quite a feat. After she got her set of wheels, though, it was nearly impossible. Once she made so many purchases I threatened to pull her battery if she didn't slow down. I'd always known she was an unstoppable woman of God, but that trip far exceeded my expectations.

Despite her illness, I never considered her confined to a wheelchair. Rather, she traveled by power chair. Super-charged from the inside out, she was amazing. She relied on God's ability instead of her own. Through her, I learned that "with God all things are possible" (Matthew 9:26). If she could conquer rheumatoid arthritis with God's help, then I could do the same with sight loss.

Janice's husband has since retired and they've moved away to the beach. However, through the miracles of email and unlimited cell phone plans we are still able to keep in touch. I've learned of the triumphs the Lord is still providing her every day. Of course, I've also heard about the obstacles she continues to face with the pain and suffering of rheumatoid arthritis, as well as the ones that are common to each of us. Her faithfulness reminds me to be faithful, too.

Perhaps you don't have a power chair. But if you are truly God's child, born of the Spirit, you have everything you need to conquer what lies before you—and then some. Through the love of Jesus, we are more than conquerors. We have the power to triumph over the hassles of today and the demands of tomorrow.

What is leaving you feeling powerless and disabled? What is keeping you spiritually paralyzed—fear, unbelief, guilt, shame, or something similar? Whatever the condition, Jesus loves you. Run to Him now and find renewal, courage, and equipping to triumph in and through it all.

Prayer

Faithful Lord, I come to You today to receive from You the power, courage, strength, and energy to withstand every difficulty that comes my way today.
I ask You to provide everything I need to overcome any and every obstacle in my life. Rise up in me with power that I might be an example to others. And even when I'm feeling weak, hopeless, and ill-equipped, supply the power I need to overcome.

Thursday
Power Tools

Brothers, think of what you were when you were called. Not many of you were wise by human standards; not many were influential; not many were of noble birth. But God chose the foolish things of the world to shame the wise; God chose the weak things of the world to shame the strong. He chose the lowly things of this world and the despised things—and the things that are not—to nullify the things that are.
1 Corinthians 1:26-28

The twelve disciples were regular Joes, ordinary men whom God used in extraordinary ways. They were the called, "the chosen," hand-picked by Jesus after a night of prayer. The stellar group included some Galilean brothers, a few fishermen, a revolutionary, and a tax collector.

When Jesus decided who would travel in ministry with Him, He did not pull from the pool of leaders in the Roman government or from the list of pillars at the local synagogue. Instead, He called commoners with the idea of teaching and training them to make an uncommon impact. Think about it. Jesus surrounded Himself with peasants. He drew from the discard pile of this world to develop a winning hand.

When I read in scripture that Jesus spent a night in prayer before naming the disciples, I have to chuckle. I wonder if it took that long for God to convince Jesus that He'd heard correctly. Did He receive His answer early on and then spend the rest of the time asking, "Are you sure about this?" I wonder if Jesus looked over the list and thought, "Okay, but what is plan B?"

From Jesus' first "Come follow me" until His ascension, the gospels record the good, the bad, and the ugly of the disciples. We don't have to read past the first four books of the New Testament for an honest account of the twelve. Included alongside their victories are their failings, foibles, and faithlessness. Like us, they were imperfect people—real and really flawed.

For three years, these men participated in Jesus' earthly ministry. They witnessed miracles, signs, and wonders. They walked and talked with Jesus. He taught them personally, often explaining the deepest truths of God, how He would not always be with them, and that they would be entrusted with taking the gospel message to the world.

After witnessing the death, resurrection, and ascension of Jesus, the motley crew of men was transformed by the Holy Spirit. Jesus' twelve closest followers became powerful forces of God whose witness and words turned the world upside down. The disciples went from being just plain to just plain extraordinary—ordinary men serving an extraordinary Lord.

Like those early disciples, we, too, are regular Joes, ordinary people God can use in extraordinary ways. They were the called and the chosen. So are we. Think about it. Just like the first disciples, we've been given the task of taking the good news of Jesus to the world. Our ordinary pursuits become extraordinary when we recognize that God is always at work and He invites us to partner with Him in what He's doing.

In God's hands, the mediocre and mundane take on the miraculous. The daily grind produces other-worldly possibilities when we view our lives through the lens of the Holy Spirit.

Grocery store outings, running errands, and mall excursions become divine appointments when we pray as we go. God may use us to encourage a cashier, a bagboy, or a fellow-shopper. When we tune in and listen to the Holy Spirit, He may impress us to phone a friend, offer a prayer for a loved one, or email someone He brings to mind. In so doing, we make an eternal difference. After the fact, we often learn that our action came at "just the right moment."

When we spend time with Jesus in His word and follow His example He can accomplish the incredible through us. Plugged into His presence, we are power tools in His skilled hands. On any given day our just plain ordinary selves can have an unending impact.

Aren't you happy that Jesus still calls common people with the idea of teaching and training them to do uncommon things? How will you make a difference today? Who will you impact for the Kingdom of God?

Prayer

Precious Lord, we offer ourselves to You this day. We ask You to take our lives in Your hands and use us powerfully to impact the lives of the people around us. As we go about our day today make us mindful of the needs of others. Use us to encourage and help others. Give us opportunities to share with others the good news of Jesus and the blessings of the Lord. We ask that You make us power tools with powerful impacts. Transform this ordinary day into an extraordinary adventure.

Friday
A Planting of the Lord's

In your hearts set apart Christ as Lord.
Always be prepared to give an answer to everyone
who asks you to give the reason for the hope that you have.
But do this with gentleness and respect.
1 Peter 3:15

When I began fourth grade, I was thrilled that my good friend, Christie, and I were to be in the same class again. I knew this was a *good* thing. Only later did I realize it was a *God* thing.

The first day of school, right away I noticed the difference in Christie. It wasn't her appearance. Though she was a little taller, she had the same silky blond hair and pretty blue eyes. Yet she seemed happier. Her smile seemed to radiate from within. I assumed she'd gone on some great vacation over summer break—Disney World maybe.

At lunch we sat together, her orange lunch tray across from mine. She was so excited I thought she would pop waiting for the opportunity for girl-talk. Before I could even open my milk carton she exclaimed, "Something great happened to me over summer break." I braced myself to hear all about Mickey and Minnie. Instead she said, "I accepted Jesus as my Lord. And that's why I'm so happy. I have Jesus in my heart." She explained how she'd gone to revival services at her church where she prayed to receive Christ and was baptized the following Sunday.

I didn't have to understand everything about church or Jesus to know I wanted what made my friend so happy. She talked about Jesus often that school year. Only ten, Christie eagerly shared the reason for the hope within her. The following summer, I prayed and asked Jesus to be my Lord, too.

Christie was an evangelist of the simplest kind, an average fourth-grader whose words and actions made an above-average impact. Because of her witness and testimony, I will spend all of eternity with Jesus. Christie was a "planting of the Lord for the display of His splendor" (Isaiah 61:3). She was a bouquet of sweet fragrance and vibrant color that conveyed the character of her great Lord. She bloomed where she was planted and I'm thankful the Lord planted her right in the middle of my fourth-grade class.

Other classmates might have thought she was nothing special, but I knew better. She was simply sensational. As is often the case when the "super" meets the "natural," something supernatural had occurred in her—repentance, forgiveness, a changed heart with a heavenly destination.

The Lord's church advances by the faithful steps of such believers, ordinary people who simply tell others about Jesus. Spreading the gospel is as natural as one beggar telling another where to get bread, one friend telling another about the reason for her hope.

Seems too easy, doesn't it? I mean, who'd have thought the preaching of Peter, an uneducated fisherman, could result in 3,000 people being saved in one day? Yet scripture tells us that's exactly what happened. When Jesus told the disciples they would do great things, He wasn't joking, was He? They healed broken people, wrote the New Testament, testified before kings and religious councils, and spread the gospel throughout the known world.

Imagine going to Priscilla and Aquila to buy a tent and getting so much more! How many lives must have been changed by their testimonies and their business practices? The greater question is this: Is our testimony and witness changing lives? Are we always ready to tell others the reason for the hope in us?

Ask yourself: Am I a planting of the Lord, displaying His splendor? Am I blooming where I'm planted at work, at home, and elsewhere?

Prayer

Father God, make us each a planting that blooms in season and out. Fill us with such passion and love for You and for others that we cannot help telling others about You. Use each of us in our own neighborhoods, workplaces, communities, and families. Let us be Your mouthpieces everywhere we go, espousing the hope You've planted within us that we might be Your planting, displaying Your splendor for all to see.

Weekend Reflections

Saturday-Sunday

Grasping the Unseen Hand

Grab your Bible, a notebook, and a pen, and let's withdraw to a quiet place for time with the Lord.

Are you caught out in a storm? Are you staring at what seems impossible? Keep your eyes on Jesus and amazing things will happen!

Read Matthew 14:22-33

- As long as Peter kept his eyes on Jesus, he could do the impossible.
- Are your eyes focused on Jesus today?

Memorize Philippians 4:13

> *I can do everything through him who gives me strength.*

Write out your reflections from today's time with the Lord.

Prayer

Lord, help me keep my eyes on You.

Week Four

Monday
Tiara Faith

The LORD your God is with you,
he is mighty to save.
He will take great delight in you,
he will quiet you with his love,
he will rejoice over you with singing.
Zephaniah 3:17

When my niece was a preschooler, she loved playing a dress-up board game called Pretty Princess. Having no daughters of my own, I had great fun with her, accessorizing myself with the girly-girl jewelry. We sometimes played the game for hours on end. That was many years ago. While I've long-since forgotten the details of that little game, I do remember a couple of things very vividly.

The first thing I recall is that my niece won every single time. What can I say? I was the kind of aunt who most enjoyed hearing her delightful giggles and squeals of victory. Another thing clear in my memory is that at the end of our marathon sessions we were both dressed like princess divas, adorned with necklaces, rings, bracelets, and tiaras.

There was one notable difference between my niece and me, though. When it came time to put the game away my niece skipped off singing happily, still confident she was a princess diva even without the baubles. Playing the game or not, she confidently owned her value. By sharp contrast, when I stuffed the tiaras and other game pieces into the box, the game was over. It was back to reality.

Interesting, isn't it? Little girls so easily own their princess status. When they put on a fairytale gown and tiara they aren't merely dressing up. They are celebrating who they are by nature. I call this tiara faith. The Bible refers to it as childlike faith—the utter and complete understanding that God loves us just because. It is the acceptance that we don't have to earn our salvation, buy His love, or wear a crown to manifest His delight in us.

The Amplified Bible, in Zephaniah 3:17, reminds us: "The Lord your God is in the midst of you, a Mighty One, a Savior [Who saves]! He will rejoice over you with joy; He will rest [in silent satisfaction] *and* in His love He will be silent *and* make no mention [of past sins, or even recall them]; He will exult over you with singing."

Good news, isn't it?

Little girls seem to get it. If you don't believe me just look around the next time you're in the grocery store, at the mall, or at church. More times than I can count I've been stopped dead in my tracks by a twirling little princess in a frilly dress dancing with delight.

To tell the truth, I have long ago vague recollections of that being me. I, too, once had tiara faith. That's the way it was before my tiara tarnished.

Our lives are peppered with emotional injuries that leave us deflated and devalued. Game over. And our princess mindset goes back in the box. We stuff deep inside the knowledge that we were created for royalty.

Do you mind if I ask about your situation? Have you lost your childlike faith? Is your tiara tarnished? Have you surrendered it and thrown it back in the box? If so, I say it's time for a change. It's time to reclaim your tiara. Jesus is your Prince. You are His chosen, His princess. You have been adopted by the King. You are part of His royal family. It's time to take up your tiara and follow Christ.

You are who God says you are and He loves you just as you are. Wouldn't it be "freeing" to forget trying to measure up to who the world says you should be? Isn't it time to get real and be real?

I don't have anything against plastic surgery as long as we aren't deceived into believing it will somehow make us better in God's eyes. The truth is, we do not have to be liposuctioned, tummy-tucked, face-lifted, or botoxed to take a seat at the King's table. God made us. He knows us. And He never intended that we be made up of ninety percent fillers. His desire is that we be filled with His Spirit and the fruit in keeping with the beauty He has given us—love, joy, peace, patience, kindness, goodness, gentleness, faithfulness, and self-control (Galatians 5:22).

I say it's time to throw off past insults and take up tiaras of faith. We are daughters of the King, born-again into Royalty, adopted into the family of God. We are princesses. Divine Divas.

Let that thought settle for a moment. When did you last think of yourself in terms of how God sees you? Why not trade in your dull and battered tiara for one that doesn't tarnish?

Begin by memorizing the verse we started with today.

The LORD your God is with you,
he is mighty to save.
He will take great delight in you,
he will quiet you with his love,
he will rejoice over you with singing.
Zephaniah 3:17

Prayer

Sweet Jesus, today we joyfully and eagerly acknowledge that we are Yours—born again into the royal family, adopted, chosen children of the King. As such, we choose to take up our tiaras of faith and follow You. Pull us more deeply into our relationship to You as You rejoice over us with singing. Let us delight in You as You quiet us with Your love.

Tuesday
Dressed to Kill

Therefore, as God's chosen people, holy and dearly loved, clothe yourselves with compassion, kindness, humility, gentleness and patience.
Bear with each other and forgive whatever grievances you may have against one another. Forgive as the Lord forgave you.
Colossians 3:12-13

Standing at the check-out counter, I used to feel inferior seeing the air-brushed images on the magazine covers. I wanted to be "dressed to kill" like those women and or the ones on TV.

Most days I feel like a candidate for being ambushed, kidnapped, and dragged onto a one of those makeover shows. Even when I try really hard, fashion blunders happen.

The first time I went back to church after the birth of my oldest son I wanted to impress someone—anyone. I'd been home for weeks and, quite frankly, I was tired of the baby getting all the attention. Every time anyone would come to the hospital or to our house they would breeze right past me to get to him. I was beginning to feel invisible. I kept hoping someone would notice *me*. But nooooo, it was all about the baby—gifts for the baby, pictures of the baby, ooohs and ahhhs for the baby.

So when I finally made it back to church I didn't want to look good, I wanted to look goooood. I took particular pains in getting ready. I walked out the door in my size four, belted, royal blue Sunday-go-to-meetin' dress feeling pretty doggone proud. I was stylin'. Nobody had to know about the stretch marks and c-section incision. That day it was all about what was on the outside.

Feeling good for all the wrong reasons, I was so high on myself I had no place to go but down. Things were going well until I guess God has seen enough. In short measure, He helped me get over myself.

During the welcome time I worked the crowd—talked to friends, laughed loudly, tossed my long curls over my shoulders—turning my little size-four self all around thinking I was all that. Then a friend whispered something in my ear. I couldn't make out what she was saying over the noise of the music and the crowd. I asked her to repeat it. She leaned in closer and began to speak louder. At that exact moment, the music and crowd silenced. In the sudden quiet, she shouted, "I SAID YOU NEED TO ADJUST YOUR DISPOSABLE NURSING PAD."

I looked down and there, sitting right at my throat like a pendent on a necklace, shone a large patch of white, publicly mocking me. It was not the accessory I'd planned for my debut. Red-faced and humbled, I slid the offending article out of sight as best I could and slunk back to my seat.

Since then I've learned I can't even pretend to have it all together. I once showed up for a day of shopping with friends wearing one black shoe and one brown. On another occasion I donned a dress that had just come back from the cleaners. A friend pulled me aside and pointed out the aluminum foil patches all down the front that had been placed there to protect the buttons. Another time I'd painstakingly put on a new outfit for a speaking engagement. When I came off the platform someone showed me the price tag dangling under one sleeve.

In my life, those things just seem to happen. They serve as opportunities for a good laugh—usually—and cause me to pause and examine what's important to me. What matters most, I've learned, is not what is on the outside, but rather what is on the inside.

Let me ask you, like me, is your outside image-challenged? But how are you clothed on the inside? Paul reminds us what we wear on the inside is as much a choice as how we clothe our outside. Check your interior wardrobe. How does it measure up to Paul's instructions in today's verse?

Choose to wear compassion, kindness, humility, gentleness, and patience. They will put you on the dressed-to-kill list every time!

Prayer

Heavenly Father, forgive me for the times I've thought too highly of myself and for the times my priorities have been out of order. Today I'm making a conscious choice to clothe myself with qualities pleasing to You—compassion, kindness, humility, gentleness, and patience. Lord, make me always mindful that attitudes are more important than what we are wearing on the outside.

Wednesday
Sole to Soul

He died for us so that, whether we are awake or asleep, we may live together with him.
Therefore encourage one another and build each other up, just as in fact you are doing.
1 Thessalonians 5:10-11

And let us consider how we may spur one another on toward love and good deeds.
Hebrews 10:24

I often marvel at the incredible soul-to-soul connection of believers. Through the indwelling Holy Spirit we have a Divine Connection that is better than DSL or 4G. Nothing compares to the link we have to others when the Lord is our Lord. He provides interactive capabilities that far exceed those of radio and sound waves.

That explains how my accountability partner knows when I'm about to embark on "binge therapy." Without fail, she calls me just before I reach for the chocolate ice cream. A word or two of encouragement from her and my true craving is satisfied. God sees and cares, so He sends Holy Spirit help in the form of a caring soul. Listening to the Spirit and reading God's Word equips us to minister in insightful ways.

My life is filled with a variety of people who are walking in the Spirit and according to God's Word. These are sisters in Christ who seem to know what I need just when I need it. I can't count the times I've walked to the mailbox and been greeted by an encouraging note. I've read it and thought, "How did she know?" and then realized it was a God thing,

Holy vibes. Days when I've felt sadly alone, I've received an invitation to lunch. I'm convinced these are touches from God sent to me by way of a spirit-inclined, spirit-filled person.

I'm surrounded by spiritual sisters, women who know Jesus as their Lord and God as their Father. These soul sisters are as varied in personality and style as the shoes in Amelda Marcos' closet yet they minister according to the leading of the Spirit and the Word.

In many ways they are a lot like shoes. You might say we have a *sole-to-soul* connection. Like shoes, they come in various shapes, sizes, and colors. They decorate my life with beauty and fun. They sometimes protect me and they always help me move in the direction I need to go, but they have individual styles and personalities. Like designer shoes, each is uniquely crafted.

We women spend a lot of time thinking about the kinds of shoes we like, don't we? I wonder, though, have you ever thought what type of shoe you're most like? Which shoes do you most resemble? Unusual question, but give it a whirl. If you're having a hard time deciding, check out these:

- The Fuzzy Slipper friend can make you laugh no matter what.
- The Soccer Shoe friend will give you a kick in the rear when needed.
- The Black Pump friend is always there with sensible suggestions.
- The Flip-flop friend wavers about EVERYTHING, including wavering.
- The Slipper Sock friend steadies you when you're about to slip and fall.

- The Ballet Slipper friend is always on her toes, quick to think and act.
- The Open-toed Heel friend is warm and friendly, transparent, very open.
- The Summer Sandal friend is carefree and fun, making any outing a vacation.
- The Fishing Wader friend enters deep waters with you to nurture and protect.
- The Evening Shoe friend is the one you call when you need late-night therapy.
- The Suede Mule friend, considered stubborn at times, is steadfast and loyal.
- The Favorite Shoe friend is your reliable "go to" person for everything.

If I were a shoe, I'd be a Stiletto—the taller the better. My theory is the higher the heel, the closer to God.

Want to get closer to God and at the same time help a friend? Take a few minutes right now to be alone with the Lord. Spend some time praying for your friends. And don't forget to thank God for your soul sisters—and especially for Jesus, a friend like no other.

Prayer

Thank You, God, for all the friends I have in my life. Thank You for the variety and giftedness of each. I ask You to show me how to be a blessing to them as they are to me. Thank You, too, for Jesus, the best friend anyone could ever have.

Thursday
Getting Rid of Stinkin' Thinkin'

Whatever is true, whatever is noble,
whatever is right, whatever is pure,
whatever is lovely, whatever is admirable—
if anything is excellent or praiseworthy—
think about such things.
Philippians 4:8

Are you your own worst enemy? Do you constantly battle a negative, defeated, or critical thought life? If so, you are not alone. I am right there with you and so are a lot of other people.

Most of us, in truth, can talk ourselves into a bad day within minutes if not seconds after first waking up. Some days I feel like spitting nails the minute my eyes open and have no explanation as to why. While I am not a morning person by nature, I do want to be excited about life without depending on a java jolt to kick-start a positive attitude. I want to enjoy the "abundant life" Jesus offers—even before I climb out from beneath the covers. I want to stay a few steps ahead of the enemy who seems to try awfully hard to pull my thoughts lower and lower as I go through my morning routine.

The question is, how can we rise above our own negative thought life to "think healthy thoughts"? What can we do to break the habit of stinkin' thinkin' once and for all?

Philippians 4:8 says, "Whatever is true, whatever is noble, whatever is right, whatever is pure, whatever is lovely, whatever is admirable—if anything is excellent or praiseworthy—think about such things." In other words,

Paul is instructing us to actively choose our thoughts, to develop a thought life that is consistent with God's word.

Did you know you can choose to realign your inner dialogue to be consistent with God's word? That's a relief, isn't it? Replacing our thoughts with God-thoughts will change our days, our lives, and our minds.

Want to begin to rid your life of the habit of stinkin' thinkin'? Begin to change your mind today by choosing to think according to God's words.

Try adopting the following thoughts, incorporating them into your day.

Today is a gift. Yesterday is gone—it's history. Tomorrow hasn't yet come—it's a mystery. What we have is now, today, the present. Today is a gift and that's why we call it—"the present." Psalm 18:24 says, "This is the day the Lord has made; let us rejoice and be glad in it."

God has a plan for my life. Begin each day by reminding yourself that God has a plan for your life that includes following His guidance day by day. Jeremiah 29:11 says, "'For I know the plans I have for you,' declares the Lord, 'plans to prosper not to harm you, plans to give you hope and a future.'" The Lord has a future planned for us that is worth getting up for every day.

Nothing can separate me from God's love. No matter what each day holds, one thing is certain—God loves you. You do not have to earn His love, buy His love, or win His love. Romans 8:38-39 says, "For I am convinced that neither death nor life, neither angels nor demons, neither the present nor the future, nor any powers, neither height nor depth, nor anything else in all creation, will be able to separate us from the love of God that is in Christ Jesus our Lord."

Prayer

God, would You rid me of stinkin' thinkin' once and for all? Replace my thoughts with Your thoughts today as I remember that this day is a gift, that You have a plan for my life, and nothing can separate me from Your love. When I am tempted to grumble and complain, remind me to think on what is good and pleasing to You.

Friday
Reckless Words

May the words of my mouth
and the meditation of my heart
be pleasing in your sight,
O LORD, my Rock and my Redeemer.
Psalm 19:14

Have you ever said something and immediately realized you said the wrong thing? I would venture to say each of us has at one time or another said something we wished we could take back before the sound waves even reached the listening ears. The most thoughtful person speaks thoughtlessly from time to time.

My father-in-law, who has since gone to be with the Lord, once told us about an embarrassing moment several years ago. He was traveling by plane on business when his dry wit and naughty sense of humor got the best of him. He offhandedly said to the baggage handler, "You'd better check that bag carefully, you know. It may explode."

Before he could explain that he merely meant to say his bag was overstuffed, swarms of men and women who looked like they'd stepped right out of the TV dramas "24" or "NCIS" surrounded my father-in-law. In no time flat he was pulled out of line and hotly interrogated, his luggage quickly confiscated and thoroughly investigated.

Everything in his suitcase was spilled out and poured over. His belongings were laid bare. Nothing was left untouched, unturned, or unchecked. Fruit of the looms were tossed like a fruit salad. Rolled socks were pitched like baseballs.

Carefully packed PJ's were held up for everyone in the airport to see.

His words set off a chain reaction. So can ours. Gossip, slander, criticism, sarcasm, hatefulness, and the like wound people to the very core. Whoever said, "Sticks and stones can break my bones, but words will never harm me," didn't know what he was talking about.

The truth is, words matter. They have the power to either tear down or build up. Our tongues can leave others injured and bleeding without our ever seeing a physical manifestation of the hurt.

In his letter, James tells us, "But no man can tame the tongue. It is a restless evil, full of deadly poison. With the tongue we praise our Lord and Father, and with it we curse men, who have been made in God's likeness. Out of the same mouth come praise and cursing. My brothers, this should not be" (James 3:8-10).

I once heard a pastor relate a story about a woman in his congregation. She had a habit of spreading gossip about him and his family. One day she went to his home and asked for forgiveness.

Realizing she did not understand the serious damage she had already caused, he told her, "I will forgive you, but first do this for me. Go home, take a feather pillow from your house, cut it up, and scatter the feathers to the wind. After you do that, come see me again."

Though puzzled by the strange request, the woman was happy to be let off with so easy a penance. She quickly cut up the pillow, scattered the feathers, and returned to his house.

"I did as you asked," she said. "Am I forgiven now?"

"Just one more thing," he said. "Go and gather up all the feathers."

"But that's impossible. The wind has already scattered them."

"Precisely," he answered. "And though you may truly wish to correct the evil you have done, it is as impossible to take back the words you have said as it is to recover the feathers."

While that story may be fictitious, the scenario is played out in our lives every day. Sometimes we hurt others with our words. At other times we are wounded by the words of others. Either way, our words can never be unsaid.

The greatest lesson we can learn from this story is to let our words be pleasing to God.

Prayer

Father God, make us always mindful of what we say. Teach us to use our words to encourage and help others. Forgive us when we say and do the wrong thing and lead us to ask for and issue forgiveness in love.

Weekend Reflections
Saturday-Sunday

Grasping the Unseen Hand

Grab your Bible, a notebook, and a pen, and let's withdraw to a quiet place for time with the Lord.

The world doesn't often send positive messages to us about who we are, does it? Did you know you were created on purpose, with purpose, and for purpose? Did you know you are divine by design and designed by the divine?

Read Psalm 139:1-18

- You are fearfully and wonderfully made
- God adores you just as you are

Memorize Psalm 139:13-14

For you created my inmost being;
you knit me together in my mother's womb.
I praise you because I am fearfully and wonderfully made; your works are wonderful, I know that full well.

Write out your reflections from today's time with the Lord.

Prayer

Thank You, Lord, that You know me completely and love me still.

Week Five

Monday
Morning Glory

Give ear to my words, O LORD, consider my sighing.
Listen to my cry for help,
my King and my God, for to you I pray.
In the morning, O LORD, you hear my voice;
in the morning I lay my requests before you
and wait in expectation.
Psalm 5:1-3

When I was a little girl, I loved helping my grandmother plant her garden. She was an experienced gardener. She'd walk slightly ahead of me over the dark rich soil. I remember holding up my cupped hands, eager to receive whatever seeds she offered. She knew exactly what needed to be planted where, so she'd give me just enough for one little hole at a time.

Thinking about my grandma's garden, I envision God holding His bag filled with every possible type of spiritual seeds, ready to dispense them to us, one at a time, at just the right moment. When we face seemingly impossible circumstances, His endless supply is available to us, just right for whatever comes our way. That's why spending time in prayer—communicating with Him—is crucial. Need a little courage? That's no problem for God. Desire wisdom? He's got that, too. Lack strength? He's all-powerful. Having a hard time loving your neighbor? Well, just think—God is love. Whatever the need, God has the seed.

You may be an ordinary person, but always remember you serve an extraordinary Lord. The "super" of God equips the "natural" in us so we can overcome. When we withdraw early in the morning to pray, we receive from God what we need to accomplish His will that day.

The old hymn, *In the Garden,* depicts the sweet interaction of the *simple* with the *Simply Divine*. The songwriter describes stealing away early in the morning to a garden spot where he meets with God. His alone time with the Lord is personal and intimate. As he lingers, he is renewed and refreshed. Lavished with love, he experiences an uncommon joy. In those private moments the *lowly* and the *Lofty* communicate.

When we kneel in our *garden spot*, though we might be as common as the dirt beneath our knees, God will empower and enable us. He did it with the first disciples and He will do it with you and me. The same God who turned the world upside down with a few garden-variety men can use you, too.

Jesus was a perfect blend of ordinary and extraordinary. He traded the comforts of Heaven to become a man. He took on human flesh, lived a life of self-sacrifice, then suffered and died a cruel death. He denied his fleshly desires, endured suffering without complaint, and conquered death with resurrection power. To accomplish all this, He often withdrew to be alone in prayer. Perhaps His most desperate pleas came in the Garden of Gethsemane just before He was crucified. Jesus' garden-spot prayer empowered Him to do the unthinkable—to offer Himself on a wooden cross unto death.

The next time you kneel in prayer, envision Jesus kneeling in the Garden of Gethsemane. There He was strengthened to be our extraordinary Savior. When He stopped in the garden, He stooped there for you and me. It is His sacrifice that re-creates us.

Remember. He knelt and prayed. He stood and went. He died and arose. He ascended and intercedes. He lives. And we are transformed.

What an extraordinary Lord!

Prayer

Lord, thank You for the mornings and for the realization that when we awake we are with You. You are attentive to our prayers. We lay our requests at Your feet and entrust every care to You. We wait expectantly for You, Lord, and for Your voice. You are our portion and You portion out to us what we need for the day in true morning glory.

Tuesday
Just Be Still

Be still and know that I am God.
Psalm 46: 10

Whatever you're facing, no matter your chaos, God has the calm you long for. Do you hear Him saying to you what He has often said to me? "Come to me, all you who are weary and burdened, and I will give you rest. Take my yoke upon you and learn from me, for I am gentle and humble in heart, and you will find rest for your souls. For my yoke is easy and my burden is light" (Matthew 11: 28-30). Stop reading for a few seconds and listen for His voice.

I don't know what you're going through, but I do know chaos. There was the time I received a phone call from my mother-in-law. She had just learned she had colon cancer and was expected to live just two short years. The news felt like a blow to my heart. Another hit came when we saw our precious little blond-haired son's MRI report showing a brain tumor. The doctors scheduled a nine-hour surgery. His uncertain future was very frightening. Years later, with teenagers in the house we faced the daily rigors of trying to protect them and relate to them. The pain of crushed dreams and relational struggles brought tremendous stress into our lives. In addition, sight loss and further retinal deterioration continued its attack on my eyesight. It seemed everything was unraveling at the seams into an impossible mess.

Yes, I've known chaos. But I've also known calm. I'm amazed that even when we're swirling in turmoil we can know the peace of God. And we can have peace with God. Something incredible happens when we learn to sit before

Him. As we turn every situation over to Him, He illumines the places that don't make sense. Though we panic, God is a constant source of refuge and comfort. He beckons us to Him. Then, in His unique way, He does what only He can do. He weaves meaning into the madness that surrounds us. He transforms the messes into messages. He forgives our mistakes and uses us in His mission fields.

He continually extends His invitation to come to Him. When I ignore Him and neglect spending time with Him, I'm in danger of developing SADD—Spiritual Attention Deficit Disorder. I don't know if you're familiar with that malady, but it's when you can't sit still long enough to give God the time He deserves. It's when you can't focus your mind on His Word enough to remember what you've read.

Do you know how it is to dress a toddler who can't be still? They wiggle and squirm, twist and turn. Sometimes I think God wants to say to me, like I've said to my boys, "Would you just hold still? Can you please stop moving long enough for me to do what I need to do?"

That is what God wants you to do in the middle of your busy-ness and craziness. Through the Psalmist, in Psalm 46:10, He says to you and me, "Be still and know that I am God." As challenges come, stop what you're doing and recognize that God is God.

Just Be Still

When the kids are loud, but you need quiet and calm, Be still and know that I am God.

When your keys are locked in the car and you're locked out, Be still and know that I am God.

When you feel there aren't enough hours to do what needs to be done, Be still and know that I am God.

When nothing you do seems good enough for anyone you know, Be still and know that I am God.
When the pressures of this world begin to close in,
Be still and know that I am God.
When your pain is great and the hurts run deep,
Be still and know that I am God.
When you are exhausted, but having another sleepless night, Be still and know that I am God.
When the job is over, but the bills still come,
Be still and know that I am God.
When the marriage has ended but your commitment to it hasn't, Be still and know that I am God.
When the diagnosis is in and "it doesn't look good"
Be still and know that I am God.
Be still,
Know that God is God.
When you wake in the morning,
When you lie down at night,
And every moment in between,
...In this moment
Just be still.

Prayer

Father, draw me into a quiet place with You and cause me to just be still.

Wednesday
Driving Ms. Donna

And my God will meet all your needs according to his glorious riches in Christ Jesus.
Philippians 4:19

Sight loss continues to teach me new things about God. Funny, isn't it? Facing the imposing darkness of blindness is what often causes me look more directly into the light God offers. He has used my visual impairment more than any other one thing in my life to shed spiritual light and to reveal important spiritual truths.

God first said, "Let there be light," thousands of years ago and He's still saying it today. Every time He reveals a new truth a spiritual light bulb shines into an otherwise darkened place.

Perhaps more than anything, I have experienced firsthand the incredible provision of the Lord. The same Jesus who fed 5,000 people with little more than an Oscar Mayer Lunchables still feeds the hungry today. The same Lord who is described as the Light of the World wants to shine light into yours. God says, "Call to me and I will answer you and tell you great and unsearchable things you do not know" (Jeremiah 33:3).

Vision loss pushed me into the passenger's seat physically. It forced me to rely on others to do things that needed to be done. I was shoved over to ride shotgun spiritually, too—to leave the driving to Jesus. I had to learn to rely on Him more and more. There was no other choice. As I yielded control to Him, I gradually learned that He had everything under control all along.

I had no frame of reference for managing my life with limited vision. Fortunately, God did. I was home alone one day thinking I was destined for a day of housework and more housework. I soon learned God had another idea in mind.

For no particular reason, I'd gotten up early that morning. After everyone else had left the house, I looked longingly out the window at my car. The engine was cold and had been that way for some time. My keys went unused. "I wish I could still drive," I thought. "If I could, I'd head straight to Uptons."

The local department store was my favorite shopping spot. This day, though, it wasn't as much about buying things as it was about going. I just wanted to get in the car and go.

Determined to keep busy, I pulled out the cleaning supplies. My mind wandered anyway. "What I wouldn't give to escape the four walls of this house for a while," I mused. "I'd roll back the sunroof and sing along with praise music on the radio." I could almost smell stale fries accidentally dropped during a previous trip to McDonald's.

With a sigh, I put away the dust cloth and pulled out the broom. I guess I was trying to sweep away my longings. I'd taken so much for granted all those years when I could come and go as I pleased. Exploring Uptons had been commonplace. Now it was a rare treat.

I sulked while I worked—and complained—and pouted. "Nobody else has to ask for rides to go places. My friends are so lucky. When they want to shop, they just get in their cars and take off."

Moving on to scrubbing the bathroom, I kept working until my thoughts quieted. The desire, however, never left. I just resigned myself to the fact that I'd have to forget the whole thing.

A couple of hours later the phone rang. A familiar voice said, "Hi, Donna. I was just wondering; would you like to go shopping with me?"

"Are you kidding?" I exclaimed without hesitation. "Yes! I've wanted to get out of the house all day long."

I was thrilled that I was going shopping, but ecstatic when my friend went on to say, "I have to make some returns. Do you mind if we go to Uptons?"

Did I *mind*? "No, that'll be fun," I said, trying to contain my excitement.

When I hung up the phone, I had my own little praise service. God had seen my desire and met me in it without my even asking. I was both humbled and amazed that the Maker of Heaven and Earth displayed His consideration of me in such a tangible way. The Need-meeter Himself was providing again. I reasoned that if God could get me to Uptons He could do anything, even light my way through the hardships of blindness.

After that gift trip to Uptons I developed a deeper hunger and longing to know God better and to love Him more deeply. I began to question Him about the difference between wants and needs. Rather than moping about places I wanted to go and couldn't, I began asking Him to provide transportation for me to go where He wanted me to go.

God would provide what I needed. I didn't think that would mean a ride to the mall anytime I wanted it, but I was sure He would give me what I needed most. In essence, I asked God to shine His light on the necessities. I trusted Him to add into my life the activities that pleased Him most.

I knew He was answering that prayer when one of my sons' Sunday school teachers called and invited me to attend a weekly community Bible study with her. She offered to drive me to the class each Wednesday. I eagerly accepted her offer.

God began to show me the difference between wants and needs. I might not have had a ride to the mall every time I wanted it, but I never missed one Wednesday morning class for lack of transportation. God was faithful to provide a ride for me that year, the next, and the next five years. In seven years, for a total of 252 days, I never missed one class for lack of transportation.

That trip to Uptons and the ensuing years of Bible study convinced me that God will truly meet every need according to His riches. Nothing is impossible for Him.

Take time today to release control of the steering wheel of your life to Jesus. Slide over into the passenger seat and prepare for the amazing. Always remember that our God can do all things.

Prayer

Father God, thank You that You meet all of our needs abundantly. Thank You for the lessons learned in the classroom of life. Bless You for Your abundant provision. Thank You for reaching down to us and taking us by the hand to lead us through the good times and the hard times. Thank You that through it all You have everything under control.

Thursday
Changing Vision Changes Everything

And without faith it is impossible to please God, because anyone who comes to him must believe that he exists and that he rewards those who earnestly seek him.
Hebrews 11:6

When first diagnosed with RP, I initially grieved over the news. But after the initial shock wore off, I went on with my normal routine. Though the doctors had diagnosed a serious problem, my vision remained stable. I pushed sight loss out of my mind and threw myself into a variety of church, community, and other activities. I was very busy—in fact, too busy.

One morning, I applied my make-up then had to start over when I realized I'd outlined my *eyes* with a mauve *lip* pencil and my *lips* with a teal *eye* pencil.

A few days later, I sprayed Scrubbing Bubbles Bathroom Cleaner on my hair. I thought it was hair spray until I heard the foaming action going to work. Fortunately, no harm was done and my hair was soap scum free!

A couple of weeks later, pulling into a parking lot, I almost ran over a woman crossing in front of my car. I simply hadn't noticed her. Slamming on the brakes and nodding an apology, I headed home immediately, too shaken to finish my errands. I chastised myself, "Donna, you have to slow down and be more careful."

Later that week I needed to go to a neighboring town to buy supplies for a church day camp. The boys and I could make it there and back in a couple of hours. The drive was a simple one. I'd made it plenty of times before. With kids' songs playing through the speakers, the boys talked and laughed cheerfully in the backseat.

The sun seemed exceptionally bright. I squinted and winced. Driving into the glare was blinding. I thought, "I can't wait to head home. The sun won't be shining in my face then."

I needed silence. I turned off the music and quieted the boys. Then I slowed the car and concentrated on my driving. The road seemed so narrow. I didn't remember the store being this far.

Entering a construction zone, I leaned forward to get closer to the windshield. I gripped the steering wheel with sweaty palms and aching fingers. I couldn't understand why it felt so frightening threading between the orange construction barrels and the oncoming traffic. Seeing was strangely strenuous.

We arrived at the store in about twice the normal drive time. My shoulders were tired and tense. My fingers hurt from gripping the steering wheel.

Once inside, my eyes were fine. I was grateful for a break from the glaring sunlight. In no time we'd located the supplies we needed, purchased them, and loaded them into the trunk.

As I pulled out onto the highway, I reassured myself, "Driving home will be easy. You won't be driving into the bright light." But I was wrong.

The forty-minute drive seemed like an eternity. A few miles into it, I developed a splitting headache. The construction barrels were still an aggravation. Feeling desperate, I decided to stop again. We found a Dairy Queen and the boys enjoyed ice cream while my eyes rested. Silently, I prayed, "Lord, I know I've been too busy lately. I'm exhausted and my eyes are fatigued. I promise I'll slow down if you just let us make it home safely."

The remainder of the drive was uneventful. At the time, I didn't attribute the difficulties I'd experienced to changing eyesight. By the end of the following week, however, I knew otherwise.

All of a sudden I noticed I was unable to see things I had been able to before. My night vision didn't allow me to see steps or curbs. With alarm, I realized I could no longer read road signs or see lines on the highway. In addition, I had holes in my line of sight. Looking through my eyes was like looking through thick lattice. Blind spots dotted my visual fields.

When I walked to the mailbox at the end of our driveway I was shocked to realize I couldn't see the basketball pole and hoop I knew stood across the street. How could something so large not be seen?

Mail in hand, I stopped at the front porch swing to think. I was stunned, beginning to grasp the magnitude of my sight loss. I remembered the parking lot episode. I'd almost run over that woman, not because I was distracted, but because I couldn't see her. I didn't want to accept the truth. Finally, all my silly mistakes made sense. My vision had changed.

Another trip to the retina specialist showed a drop in both my peripheral and central vision. The doctor described it as "significant." She told me I was "no longer safe" to drive and advised me to give up the car keys forever.

An internal dialogue ensued. What? Are you joking? Me? Stop driving? Maybe I'll get a second opinion. There has to be another choice! But I knew I was pleading my case to no avail.

When we left the doctor's office I felt assaulted. My body ached with the blow of the news. Driving was a vital part of my life and ministry. I wondered how I could possibly be of benefit to either God or others if I couldn't drive.

What would I do with my time? I grieved the loss of freedom and the feeling of control. I couldn't imagine never getting behind the wheel and starting the engine again.

The change in my vision changed everything.

Reluctantly, I relinquished the keys. I was home most of the time. Don went to work and the boys went to school. I spent days feeling lonely and isolated. The doctor's stinging words played over and over in my mind. I was depressed. I felt sorry for myself. I moaned and complained.

When I stopped driving I lost something I loved. I had to readjust both my schedule and my mindset. Instead of getting in the car to go and do, I began to pull out my Bible to sit and listen.

As I spent more time alone with Jesus, I began to view the moments with Him as precious. I was not alone. I was at home with the God of the Universe.

I made a decision to stop feeling sorry for myself and to embrace the time with God. The Holy Spirit drew me toward living from the position of sitting at Jesus' feet.

Daily sitting at the feet of Jesus through prayer and God's word, I soon learned that giving up driving paled in comparison to the pleasure of knowing Him better. I found that spending time with Jesus brought peace and purpose I had not discovered until forced to be quiet.

Paul said, "What is more, I consider everything a loss compared to the surpassing greatness of knowing Christ Jesus my Lord" (Philippians 3: 8). I agreed.

Spending time with Jesus gives peace and purpose not found elsewhere. His presence is the reward of those who earnestly seek Him.

Prayer

Sweet Jesus, what a grand and glorious reward You are to those who seek You. May we each take time daily to sit at Your feet learning, listening, and loving. Nothing compares to the surpassing greatness of knowing You as Savior and Lord.

Friday
Secrets Revealed

So do not fear, for I am with you;
do not be dismayed, for I am your God.
I will strengthen you and help you;
I will uphold you with my righteous right hand.
Isaiah 41:10

When unexpected loss comes into your life are you able to look beyond the surface issues to deeper and more significant truths? Do you find rest in Christ and wait on Him to share secrets revealed when the shadows of life fall all around?

Now that I view life through blind spots, cloudy vision, and aching eyes, I look more intently for those mysteries that lie within affliction.

I am reminded of an old joke.

Sherlock Holmes and Dr. Watson went on a camping trip. After a good meal, they lay down for the night and went to sleep. Some hours later, Holmes awoke and nudged his faithful friend.

"Watson, look up at the sky and tell me what you see."

Watson replied, "I see millions and millions of stars."

"What does that tell you?" Holmes asked.

Watson pondered for a minute. "Astronomically, it tells me there are millions of galaxies and potentially billions of planets. Astrologically, I observe that Saturn is in Leo. Horologically, I deduce that the time is approximately a quarter past three. Theologically, I can see that God is all-powerful and He is high above all else. Meteorologically, I suspect that we will have a beautiful day tomorrow. What does it tell you?"

Holmes considered Watson's response then said, "My dear Watson, don't you see? Somebody has stolen our tent!"

Sherlock Holmes, of course is the natural hero, but I'm quite partial to Watson's assessment of the situation. When the tent went missing, he saw that God was all-powerful and high above all else. I think that is a great deduction for us, too.

God is all-powerful and He is high above any difficulty we will ever experience. When we walk hand-in-unseen-hand with God we can trust Him—even when He takes us to unexpected destinations.

Oh, sure, we will sometimes follow Him into the joys of graduation, engagement, marriage, childbirth, a great job, and the like. On other occasions, we hold God's hand and follow Him through job loss, parental struggles, financial strain, serious illness, death, and other shadowy life situations.

Has your tent gone missing? The good news is that suffering, though it comes with a price, brings knowledge deeper than we could imagine.

While the joys of life reveal secrets of light, pleasure, and happiness, the secrets revealed in the shadows of life are deep truths and insightful treasures. Those who faithfully persevere in faith through hard times discover the fellowship of Christ. He is the greatest secret of all.

As my vision continues to diminish I am determined to hold more tightly than ever to God's unseen hand. With each drop in my eyesight, I am more desperate to know the secrets that Jesus knew, the ones that allowed Him to conquer sin, the cross, and death. I want to share in the understanding of resurrection power and ascension astonishment. I want to run the race marked out for me and still manage to keep the faith. I want to walk by faith, not by sight, right into the loving arms of my waiting savior.

Until then, I commit to staying focused on the secrets revealed in the shadows of life, those found in Isaiah 41:10 which says, "So do not fear, for I am with you; do not be dismayed, for I am your God. I will strengthen you and help you; I will uphold you with my righteous right hand."

Do you see the wonderful secrets revealed in these verses?

- God is with you
- God is your God
- God will strengthen you
- God will help you
- God will uphold you with His unseen hand

With His righteous unseen hand He will care for us in both the joys and shadows of life. So let me ask you, when you look up, my dear friend, what do you see? An all-powerful God who is above all else is reaching out to you. It's time to take hold and hang on as He reveals great and unsearchable things.

Prayer

Most High God, we worship and adore You. You truly are high above all else. We look to You and ask You to show us how to see beneath the surface into the deeper things of the Spirit. Pull back the veil and let us experience the mysteries and secrets found only in You.

Weekend Reflections

Saturday-Sunday

Grasping the Unseen Hand

Grab your Bible, a notebook, and a pen, and let's withdraw to a quiet place for time with the Lord.

Would you like to improve your prayer life? It's as easy as releasing, receiving, and re-gifting.

Read Matthew 26:36-44

- Release your cares and concerns to God.
- Receive from Him what you need for the day.
- Re-gift what God has given you by giving out to those you meet today.

Memorize Philippians 4:6-7

Do not be anxious about anything, but in everything, by prayer and petition, with thanksgiving, present your requests to God. And the peace of God, which transcends all understanding, will guard your hearts and your minds in Christ Jesus.

Write out your reflections from today's time with the Lord.

Prayer

Thank You, Lord, that You always hear me when I pray.

Week Six

Monday
"Gotta" Meltdown

As the deer pants for streams of water,
so my soul pants for you, my God.
My soul thirsts for God, for the living God.
When can I go and meet with God?
Psalm 42:1-2

It was not my finest moment.

My "got to do" list was overwhelming. On it were all of the normal things of life like cooking, cleaning, shopping, making calls, sending notes, and caring for family. Then there were the extras, the fun things, like lunch with a friend and Friday night out with Don. Added to these were the "gottas" of ministry—gotta post on Facebook, gotta write a new blog, gotta send post cards, gotta develop new messages, and more. By midweek, I was more than a little overwhelmed. Finally, the "gottas" resulted in an emotional meltdown and a physical shut down.

The "gottas" had become "gotchas" and I was a mess. I cried real tears as I cried out in prayer to the Lord. "Lord, show me the true 'gottas'". What are the things you want me to do first? Most?"

I sat quietly until an inaudible, yet clear, voice spoke simply, "Psalm 42."

Before I could find the passage, the doorbell rang and I was on to the next thing. The rest of the day was filled with demands. I fell into bed that night without another thought of the whispered Word.

When I awoke, my mind raced immediately to the "gottas" of the day. Then there it was again, the inaudible whisper reminded me, "Psalm 42."

I rolled out of bed, grabbed my iPhone and listened to the first couple of verses.

As the deer pants for streams of water,
so my soul pants for you, my God.
My soul thirsts for God, for the living God.
When can I go and meet with God?
Psalm 42:1-2

I pressed the pause button and let the words saturate my parched soul.

"Ah, Lord, I see now. I get it. The first and most important 'gotta' is to get to you, to meet with You, God, and to drink from streams that will never run dry."

Dear Friend, let me ask you, what is on your "got to do" list today? Why not put, right at the top, "gotta get to Jesus?"

Prayer

Father God, I ask you to satisfy my hunger and thirst today. Let me always seek you first and trust you always to order out the steps of my day.

Tuesday
What $12.50 Taught Me

Each of you should give what you have decided in your heart to give, not reluctantly or under compulsion, for God loves a cheerful giver.
2 Corinthians 9:7

Don and I left Planet Fitness joking about our love-hate relationship with the elliptical. On the way home we debated whether to kill our workout with a chocolate shake.

About that time, Don strained to get a clearer look at something on the roadside. He said, "That looked like someone pushing a wheelchair!"

I thought Don was exercise delirious until he confirmed, "Yep, there's a man pushing a wheelchair, all right, and the woman in it is holding two paper sacks."

We pulled off the busy highway to the safety of a side street. We waited for the man and woman to make their way to us. As they drew closer to our car, I felt a little uneasy. I wanted to help them but was more than a little nervous about stopping.
"Don," I cautioned, "These are total strangers. Be careful." Always the Good Samaritan, Don hopped out of the car.

As he chatted with them, I wondered what this couple was doing out on such a dark night. What could they be up to? Don talked easily with the two and quickly offered them a ride to wherever they were going.

The man straightened long enough to say, “No, don’t need a ride. We’re almost there, but could you spare $12.50?” Don told him we didn’t have any cash.

The woman sat helplessly in the chair. Her husband mumbled something about an appointment, said he was headed to the McDonald’s to get a job, and mentioned the $12.50 again.

When Don climbed back into the car, we drove away but neither of us felt right about doing nothing to help. Oh sure, I admit I was a little afraid when we first stopped. I thought, “This is how good folks get robbed and beaten or worse.”

I was suddenly ashamed I’d been so suspicious.
After all, the man hadn’t asked for much, had he? Just $12.50. Little more than the cost of a couple of shakes and maybe even a little less than a couple of Venti® Starbucks drinks.

With that in mind, Don and I headed to a nearby bank. We withdrew a few dollars and went to the McDonald’s in search of the pair. When we pulled into the parking lot, Don spotted the gentleman. The two shook hands and Don said, “This isn’t much, but I hope it helps.”
The man took the single bill and explained his last paycheck from his previous job would be in the mail by the first of the week.
Once home, the cynic in me returned, “You know, Don, he may have been lying to us, may use the money for drugs. Or, we may drive past them tomorrow and find her pushing him!”

The minute the words left my lips, I wanted to take them back. I wanted to be more trusting and generous, willing to give without asking so many questions—like the elderly stranger in overalls who'd helped my friend Lisa when she needed it most.

Lisa and her little girl, Maddie, were suddenly on their own. Now, a single mom, Lisa struggled to pay the bills and also buy food and other necessities.

Once when they were grocery shopping, Lisa walked the aisles watching her small cart fill quickly. She knew she had only a few dollars in her purse and wondered how she was going to pay for everything they needed. When she got almost to the register, she prepared herself to put some items back.
With only one customer in line ahead of her now, Lisa bit her lip, fighting back the tears. Maddie twirled in circles and sang the "Hokey, Pokey." Lisa nodded absently to an elderly man in overalls who stooped to say something to Maddie.

When he walked away, Maddie lifted her little hand and opened her fist to reveal a wad of money.

Lisa's eyebrows raised as Maddie exclaimed, "That old man said 'God told me to give this to you.'"

"God told me to give this to you."
The elderly gentleman's words ran through my mind. I suddenly despised my own selfishness. I wondered how often I'd missed an opportunity to help someone because I was too distracted to see the need, too frightened to take the risk, or just didn't have any cash on me.

With that, I made a decision to lift my eyes, to be willing to show courage, and to keep a little cash on hand—just in case.

Prayer

Today, Lord, I ask you to use me. Let me be the one who says to a soul in need, "God told me to give this to you."

Wednesday
It's Okay to Cry

When Jesus saw her weeping, and the Jews who had come along with her also weeping, he was deeply moved in spirit and troubled.
John 11:33

Do you ever feel like God made a mistake when He made you? Like maybe He created you at five o'clock on Friday?

Sometimes I struggle to find significance and to get a grip emotionally. I have lived in a home with all males since I got married and had first one, then another, and yet a third son. Don't get me wrong, I love our boys. They have been a source of joy even when they've kept me on my knees, when they were young, on my knees playing, and in their teens, on my knees praying…praying…and then praying some more. Ah, but that's a story for another day.

Today, I'm thinking about being an emotional female in a Y chromosome world.

The other day I said to one of my sons, "All of a sudden I feel like crying."

Lifting his eyes from his laptop, he looked as helpless as an ant trying to lift an elephant. He didn't have to say a word. I knew what he was thinking.
"Mom is being more weird than normal and I have no idea what to say."

When he didn't say anything right away, I asked, "Do you ever feel like crying for no reason?"

He looked like he'd rather be someplace, any place else. I'm guessing he was silently counting the number of steps to get past me as soon as possible. Raising his eyebrow, he finally said, "Well, ah, no."

"You sure are lucky," I said as I turned to leave the room.

Seriously, wouldn't it be nice to never feel sad without knowing where the sadness is coming from? And, wouldn't it be easier if we women were just a little less emotional? Like, maybe it would be good if I didn't tear up every time a Publix Thanksgiving ad plays.

On the other hand, I like feeling deeply. I think that is something we have in common with Jesus.

Have you ever thought about the emotions Jesus shows in Scripture?

He wept at Lazarus' graveside. He was angry when the temple was converted to a strip mall. He prayed passionately. He restored tenderly. And, He loved deeply, so deeply that He breathed His last breath for us. For you. For me.

The next time you feel like crying for no reason, or for good reason, think of Jesus and give yourself a break. After all, you may be reacting more like Him than you've ever thought.

Prayer

Thank you, Lord, for creating us with the capacity to laugh out loud, to cry when we need to, and to love deeply.

Thursday
One Small Gift

Taking the five loaves and the two fish and looking up to heaven, he gave thanks and broke the loaves. Then he gave them to the disciples, and the disciples gave them to the people. They all ate and were satisfied, and the disciples picked up twelve basketfuls of broken pieces that were left over.
Matthew 14:19b-20

Have you ever felt like God totally skipped over you when He was handing out gifts and talents? Ever questioned whether Jesus Himself could do anything with what little you have to offer?

There was a young boy who lived a couple thousand years ago who, I bet, felt the same way.

He probably felt quite small and insignificant in the crowd of thousands, some say as many as 12,000. These folks had traveled from miles and miles around and were gathered on a hillside listening to Jesus teach.

When evening drew near, the disciples wanted to send the people away to buy food, but Jesus said to Philip, "You give them something to eat."

Philip looked around at the impossible situation. He quickly calculated how much money that would take. Andrew, another disciple, spotted a boy who had a few loaves and fishes. He brought the boy to Jesus.

Can you imagine? The youngster was practically invisible one minute and standing before the Master Himself the next. The child didn't have much but he gave what he had to Jesus.

Jesus held the loaves and fishes in His capable hands—hands that had gestured emphatically when He taught, hands that had healed the sick earlier in the day. Now, those same hands held what amounted to little more than a tuna fish sandwich. What would He do with it?

Can you imagine this little boy's excitement? His wide-eyed wonder and anticipation? He watched as Jesus gave thanks and began to break the bread. Jesus broke and broke and broke, until everyone ate to their fill and were satisfied—and there were twelve baskets of food left over.

This little boy's small gift in the hands of Jesus made a big difference. Our small gift in the hands of a big God, can make a big difference too.

Our gift…

His hands.

Hands that are more than the hands of a babe in a manger, more than the hands of a boy at the temple, more than the hands of a teen in a carpenter's shop, more than the hands of a man on a cross.

His hands…

God's hands come to earth. They are hands that multiply, hands that minister, hands that are mighty — Majestic hands.

In His hands, our small gifts can make a big difference. What small gift will you offer to Jesus today that, with His hands, will satisfy the hunger needs of others?

Prayer

Lord, I give all that I have and all that I am to You. Take that which amounts to not much more than a tuna fish sandwich and use it to feed the multitudes. Multiply my small gift in the grasp of Your mighty hand. I look forward with anticipation to how you will multiply and minister in mighty ways.

Friday
Bring a Gift of Laughter

Bring a gift of laughter,
sing yourselves into his presence.
Psalm 100:2 (MSG)

When my friend, Kathy, experienced hair loss due to chemotherapy she was strong in more ways than I can record. Her courage was remarkable, to say the least. She stood tall through her diagnosis, surgery, and chemo treatments. She bought a couple of wigs as she tried to prepare for inevitable hair loss.

Despite her best efforts, she was understandably saddened as her dark brunette mane thinned. She soon realized the full measure of the loss. She struggled to keep her composure and was visibly upset. She wondered if her husband, Mike, would still find her attractive; he wondered how he might somehow cheer her.

Mike had always been a jokester with a gift for bringing laughter into situations at just the right time. Once after Kathy had taken her wig off for the day, Mike saw it lying on the bed and couldn't resist. He slid the hair over his own balding scalp and danced his way into the kitchen where Kathy sat eating a bedtime snack. When she saw him enter the room mimicking the moves of JLo, Kathy smiled. As he continued toward her singing... "*Hey sista, go sista, soul sista, flow sista...*", Kathy almost fell out of her chair laughing.

For the first time in a long time, Kathy's worry melted into giggles and she felt normal. The moment wouldn't last forever but it gave them the umph to take the next step.

Mike brought the gift of laughter and with it a healthy release in a tense moment.

Laughter is good medicine.

Laughter has helped me cope in difficult situations all my life. God has given me a quirky sense of humor and a mind that often travels to a funny thought, memory, or story.

Like the time my son, Ben, called to say he was dropping by our house on his way to work. He said his ETA was about fifteen minutes. I was working and not paying much attention to the time so when the doorbell rang, I naturally assumed it was him standing there with his ten month old son.

In an effort to sprinkle a little joy and evoke a little laugh, I swung the door open wide and in typical *me* fashion gave a more-cheerful-than-usual and quite enthusiastic greeting.

"Come on in, you sweet thing!"

Oddly, there was no response, so I tried again.

With even greater fanfare than before I went on, "Well what are you waiting for, Handsome? Come on in."

Still nothing. That's when I realized this person was not Ben at all. Instead, standing there before me was a UPS driver who was making a delivery.

Mortified, I blubbered, “I’m so sorry. I was expecting someone else. Er, ah, I mean, my son is stopping by and I thought you were him.”

He stood quietly while I rambled on, "You see, I don’t see well so I didn’t actually see who was standing in the doorway.”

I could hear his amusement as he said, “That’s ok. No worries.”

He showed me where to sign while I kept talking, “I bet you thought I was crazy or something.”

“No, I just thought your were real, REAL friendly.”

He turned to leave and then looked back and laughed lightly, “Besides, I was kinda flattered you called me handsome, that is until, I realized you can’t actually *see* me.”

I carried the package inside, laughing all the while. A few minutes later when Ben finally arrived, I told him what happened and we laughed again.

Sometimes life is so hard we really do have to laugh to keep from crying, laugh to keep on keeping on, and laugh because it just feels good to laugh. One of my friends makes it a practice to watch something funny on her iPad every night before she goes to bed. She says it gives her a better night’s sleep and gives her something to smile about the next morning.

I think it pleases God when we throw cares aside and toss our heads back to laugh. And, I am certain it confounds the devil when we find joy despite pain and suffering.

While suffering and lightheartedness don't seem to go together, I've found that when I live with a deep recognition that God is on the throne, completely in control, I can laugh hard, laugh often and laugh out loud.

The writer of Ecclesiastes says there is a time to laugh and a time to cry. The Psalmist says that weeping lasts for a night but joy comes in the morning. He also encourages us to bring a gift of laughter to the Lord. It's ok to cry; but today, why not give yourself or someone else the gift of laughter. It'll make you feel better and it will keep the devil wondering how you can be lighthearted despite his best efforts.

On your feet now—applaud GOD!
Bring a gift of laughter,
sing yourselves into his presence.

Know this: GOD is God, and God, GOD.
He made us; we didn't make him.
We're his people, his well-tended sheep.

Enter with the password: "Thank you!"
Make yourselves at home, talking praise.
Thank him. Worship him.

For GOD is sheer beauty,
all-generous in love,
loyal always and ever.
Psalm 100 (MSG)

Prayer

Lord Jesus, stir in us the gift of laughter, today. Let us use it to encourage and strengthen the people around us who are suffering or hurting. As we rejoice and celebrate in you, let us bring with us shouts of joy and take to others the gift of laughter.

Weekend Reflections
Saturday-Sunday

Grasping the Unseen Hand

Grab your Bible, a notebook, and a pen, and let's withdraw to a quiet place for time with the Lord.

Who are you? What do you look like? What three words best describe your personality?

Read Ephesians 1:1-14

This weekend, lay aside who the world says you are and what other people have said to or about you. Focus instead on who God says you are and what His word says about you.

Below is a list of who you are in Christ from A to Z. As you read through the list below, thank God for what He has done for you through Jesus Christ. Embrace who you are as His new creation.

Adopted
Beloved
Chosen
Daughter
Equipped
Forgiven
Gifted
His Bride
Instructed
Justified
Known
Loved
More Than A Conqueror
Not Condemned
Over-comer
Precious
Quieted By His Love
Redeemed
Saved
Transformed
Under The Blood
Victorious
Washed
X-tra Special
Yoked With Christ
Zoned *Off-Limits* To The Enemy

Memorize Ephesians 1:4-6

> *For he chose us in him before the creation of the world to be holy and blameless in his sight. In love he predestined us for adoption to sonship through Jesus Christ, in accordance with his pleasure and will— to the praise of his glorious grace, which he has freely given us in the One he loves.*

Write out your reflections from today's time with the Lord.

Prayer

Thank You, Lord, for reminding of who I am in Christ. May I always see myself through your eyes and not through the eyes of the world. Thank you that I am yours from A to Z.

Bible Reference Section

This section includes scriptures that correspond to some of my most requested speaking topics. These passages have been an encouragement to me in my daily walk with the Lord and I pray they will be helpful to you as well. Turn to these pages as a quick reference guide when you are in need of:

- Finding Hope
- Finding Rest
- Finding Yourself
- Finding Joy
- Finding Strength

Finding Hope

I call out to the Lord,
and he answers me from his holy mountain
Psalm 3:4

The righteous cry out, and the Lord hears them;
he delivers them from all their troubles.
Psalm 34:17

...call on me in the day of trouble;
I will deliver you, and you will honor me.
Psalm 50:15

Trust in the Lord with all your heart
and lean not on your own understanding;
in all your ways submit to him,
and he will make your paths straight.
Proverbs 3:5-6

Seek the Lord while he may be found;
call on him while he is near.
Isaiah 55:6

Why, my soul, are you downcast?
Why so disturbed within me?
Put your hope in God,
for I will yet praise him,
my Savior and my God
Psalm 42:5

I cried out to him with my mouth;
his praise was on my tongue.

If I had cherished sin in my heart,
the Lord would not have listened;
but God has surely listened
and has heard my prayer.
Praise be to God,
who has not rejected my prayer
or withheld his love from me!
Psalm 66:17-20

Blessed are those whose help is the God of Jacob,
whose hope is in the Lord their God.
He is the Maker of heaven and earth,
the sea, and everything in them—
he remains faithful forever.
Psalm 146:5-6

About midnight Paul and Silas were praying and singing hymns to God, and the other prisoners were listening to them.
Acts 16:25

Now to him who is able to do immeasurably more than all we ask or imagine, according to his power that is at work within us, to him be glory in the church and in Christ Jesus throughout all generations, for ever and ever! Amen.
Ephesians 3:20-21

And God is able to bless you abundantly, so that in all things at all times, having all that you need, you will abound in every good work.
2 Corinthians 9:8

He has delivered us from such a deadly peril, and he will deliver us again. On him we have set our hope that he will continue to deliver us,
2 Corinthians 1:10

For he has rescued us from the dominion of darkness and brought us into the kingdom of the Son he loves,
Colossians 1:13

We have this hope as an anchor for the soul, firm and secure. It enters the inner sanctuary behind the curtain, where our forerunner, Jesus, has entered on our behalf. He has become a high priest forever, in the order of Melchizedek.
Hebrews 6:19-20

Blessed is the one who perseveres under trial because, having stood the test, that person will receive the crown of life that the Lord has promised to those who love him.
James 1:12

Consider it pure joy, my brothers and sisters, whenever you face trials of many kinds, because you know that the testing of your faith produces perseverance. Let perseverance finish its work so that you may be mature and complete, not lacking anything.
James 1:2-4

It was good for me to be afflicted
so that I might learn your decrees.
The law from your mouth is more precious to me
than thousands of pieces of silver and gold.

Psalm 119:71-72

I know, Lord, that your laws are righteous,
and that in faithfulness you have afflicted me.
May your unfailing love be my comfort,
according to your promise to your servant.
Psalm 119:75-76

And we boast in the hope of the glory of God. Not only so, but we also glory in our sufferings, because we know that suffering produces perseverance; perseverance, character; and character, hope. And hope does not put us to shame, because God's love has been poured out into our hearts through the Holy Spirit, who has been given to us.
Romans 5:2b-5

And we know that in all things God works for the good of those who love him, who have been called according to his purpose.
Romans 8:28

Finding Rest

Come to me, all you who are weary and burdened, and I will give you rest. Take my yoke upon you and learn from me, for I am gentle and humble in heart, and you will find rest for your souls. For my yoke is easy and my burden is light.
Matthew 11:28-30

By the seventh day God had finished the work he had been doing; so on the seventh day he rested from all his work. Then God blessed the seventh day and made it holy, because on it he rested from all the work of creating that he had done.
Genesis 2:2-3

In peace I will lie down and sleep,
for you alone, Lord,
make me dwell in safety.
Psalm 4:8

You will keep in perfect peace
those whose minds are steadfast,
because they trust in you.
Isaiah 26:3

The Lord is my shepherd, I lack nothing.
He makes me lie down in green pastures,
he leads me beside quiet waters,
he refreshes my soul.
He guides me along the right paths
for his name's sake.
Even though I walk

through the darkest valley,[a]
I will fear no evil,
for you are with me;
your rod and your staff,
they comfort me.
You prepare a table before me
in the presence of my enemies.
You anoint my head with oil;
my cup overflows.
Surely your goodness and love will follow me
all the days of my life,
and I will dwell in the house of the Lord
forever.
Psalm 23

I have told you these things, so that in me you may have peace. In this world you will have trouble. But take heart! I have overcome the world.
John 16:33

Do not be anxious about anything, but in every situation, by prayer and petition, with thanksgiving, present your requests to God. And the peace of God, which transcends all understanding, will guard your hearts and your minds in Christ Jesus.
Philippians 4:6-7

Peace I leave with you; my peace I give you. I do not give to you as the world gives. Do not let your hearts be troubled and do not be afraid.
John 14:27

Let the peace of Christ rule in your hearts, since as members of one body you were called to peace. And be thankful.
Colossians 3:15

He says, "Be still, and know that I am God;
I will be exalted among the nations,
I will be exalted in the earth."
Psalm 46:10

Cast all your anxiety on him because he cares for you.
1 Peter 5:7

Peacemakers who sow in peace reap a harvest of righteousness.
James 3:18

The LORD gives strength to his people; the LORD blesses his people with peace.
Psalm 29:11

Great peace have those who love your law, and nothing can make them stumble.
Psalm 119:165

Finding Yourself

The Lord does not look at the things people look at. People look at the outward appearance, but the Lord looks at the heart.
1 Samuel 16:7b

Therefore, if anyone is in Christ, the new creation has come:[a] The old has gone, the new is here!
2 Corinthians 5:17

This is what the Lord says:
"Let not the wise boast of their wisdom
or the strong boast of their strength
or the rich boast of their riches,
but let the one who boasts boast about this:
that they have the understanding to know me,
that I am the Lord, who exercises kindness,
justice and righteousness on earth,
for in these I delight,"
declares the Lord.
Jeremiah 9:23-24

Then God said, "Let us make mankind in our image, in our likeness, so that they may rule over the fish in the sea and the birds in the sky, over the livestock and all the wild animals, and over all the creatures that move along the ground."
So God created mankind in his own image,
in the image of God he created them;
male and female he created them.
Genesis 1:26-27

You have searched me, Lord,

and you know me.
You know when I sit and when I rise;
you perceive my thoughts from afar.
You discern my going out and my lying down;
you are familiar with all my ways.
Before a word is on my tongue
you, Lord, know it completely.
Psalm 139:1-4

For you created my inmost being;
you knit me together in my mother's womb.
I praise you because I am fearfully and wonderfully made;
your works are wonderful,
I know that full well.
My frame was not hidden from you
when I was made in the secret place,
when I was woven together in the depths of the earth.
Your eyes saw my unformed body;
all the days ordained for me were written in your book
before one of them came to be
Psalm 139:13-16

See what great love the Father has lavished on us, that we should be called children of God!
1 John 3:1a

Yet to all who did receive him, to those who believed in his name, he gave the right to become children of God—
John 1:12

he predestined us for adoption to sonship through Jesus Christ, in accordance with his pleasure and will—
Ephesians 1:5

Accept one another, then, just as Christ accepted you, in order to bring praise to God.
Romans 15:7

But whoever is united with the Lord is one with him in spirit.
1 Corinthians 6:17

For we know that our old self was crucified with him so that the body ruled by sin might be done away with, that we should no longer be slaves to sin—
Romans 6:6

Now you are the body of Christ, and each one of you is a part of it.
1 Corinthians 12:27

But you are a chosen people, a royal priesthood, a holy nation, God's special possession, that you may declare the praises of him who called you out of darkness into his wonderful light.
1 Peter 2:9

for all of you who were baptized into Christ have clothed yourselves with Christ. There is neither Jew nor Gentile, neither slave nor free, nor is there male and female, for you are all one in Christ Jesus.
Galatians 3:27-28

Finding Joy

Rejoice in the Lord always. I will say it again: Rejoice!
Philippians 4:4

But let all who take refuge in you be glad;
let them ever sing for joy.
Spread your protection over them,
that those who love your name may rejoice in you.
Psalm 5:11

Rejoice always,
1 Thessalonians 5:16

I rejoice in your promise
like one who finds great spoil.
Psalm 119:162

For you make me glad by your deeds, Lord;
I sing for joy at what your hands have done.
Psalm 92:4

Rejoice in the Lord and be glad, you righteous;
sing, all you who are upright in heart!
Psalm 32:11

Sing, Daughter Zion;
shout aloud, Israel!
Be glad and rejoice with all your heart,
Daughter Jerusalem!
Zephaniah 3:14

Rejoice in the Lord always. I will say it again: Rejoice!

Philippians 4:4

May the nations be glad and sing for joy,
for you rule the peoples with equity
and guide the nations of the earth.
Psalm 67:4

Shout for joy to the Lord, all the earth.
Psalm 100:1

Once more the humble will rejoice in the Lord;
the needy will rejoice in the Holy One of Israel.
Isaiah 29:19

Sing joyfully to the Lord, you righteous;
it is fitting for the upright to praise him
Psalm 33:1

But may the righteous be glad
and rejoice before God;
may they be happy and joyful.
Psalm 68:3

May the God of hope fill you with all joy and peace as you trust in him, so that you may overflow with hope by the power of the Holy Spirit.
Romans 15:13

Though you have not seen him, you love him; and even though you do not see him now, you believe in him and are filled with an inexpressible and glorious joy,
1 Peter 1:8

Glory in his holy name;

let the hearts of those who seek the Lord rejoice.
Psalm 105:3

You make known to me the path of life;
you will fill me with joy in your presence,
with eternal pleasures at your right hand.
Psalm 16:11

...weeping may stay for the night,
but rejoicing comes in the morning.
Psalm 30:5b

Those who go out weeping, carrying seed to sow, will return with songs of joy, carrying sheaves with them.
Psalm 126:6

Speak to one another with psalms, hymns, and spiritual songs. Sing and make music in your hearts to the Lord, always giving thanks to God the Father for everything in the name of our Lord Jesus Christ....
Ephesians 5:19-20

Therefore, since we are surrounded by such a great cloud of witnesses, let us throw off everything that hinders and the sin that so easily entangles. And let us run with perseverance the race marked out for us, 2 fixing our eyes on Jesus, the pioneer and perfecter of faith. For the joy set before him he endured the cross, scorning its shame, and sat down at the right hand of the throne of God. 3 Consider him who endured such opposition from sinners, so that you will not grow weary and lose heart.
Hebrews 12:1-2

The Spirit of the Sovereign Lord is on me,
because the Lord has anointed me
to proclaim good news to the poor.
He has sent me to bind up the brokenhearted,
to proclaim freedom for the captives
and release from darkness for the prisoners,[a]
to proclaim the year of the Lord's favor
and the day of vengeance of our God,
to comfort all who mourn,
and provide for those who grieve in Zion—
to bestow on them a crown of beauty
instead of ashes,
the oil of joy
instead of mourning,
and a garment of praise
instead of a spirit of despair.
They will be called oaks of righteousness,
a planting of the Lord
for the display of his splendor
Isaiah 61:1-3

Finding Strength

He gives strength to the weary
and increases the power of the weak.
Even youths grow tired and weary,
and young men stumble and fall;
but those who hope in the Lord
will renew their strength.
They will soar on wings like eagles;
they will run and not grow weary,
they will walk and not be faint.
Isaiah 40:29-31

God is my refuge and strength, a very present help in trouble.
Psalm 46:1

Nehemiah said, "Go and enjoy choice food and sweet drinks, and send some to those who have nothing prepared. This day is holy to our Lord. Do not grieve, for the joy of the Lord is your strength."
Nehemiah 8:10

I pray that the eyes of your heart may be enlightened in order that you may know the hope to which he has called you, the riches of his glorious inheritance in his holy people, and his incomparably great power for us who believe. That power is the same as the mighty strength he exerted when he raised Christ from the dead and seated him at his right hand in the heavenly realms,
Ephesians 1:18-20

I can do all this through him who gives me strength.

Philippians 4:13

But he said to me, "My grace is sufficient for you, for my power is made perfect in weakness." Therefore I will boast all the more gladly about my weaknesses, so that Christ's power may rest on me. That is why, for Christ's sake, I delight in weaknesses, in insults, in hardships, in persecutions, in difficulties. For when I am weak, then I am strong.

2 Corinthians 12:9-10

My flesh and my heart may fail,
but God is the strength of my heart
and my portion forever.
Psalm 73:26

For the Spirit God gave us does not make us timid, but gives us power, love and self-discipline.
2 Timothy 1:7

But the Lord is faithful, and he will strengthen you and protect you from the evil one.
2 Thessalonians 3:3

I love you, Lord, my strength.
The Lord is my rock, my fortress and my deliverer;
my God is my rock, in whom I take refuge,
my shield and the horn of my salvation, my stronghold.
Psalm 18:1-2

But I will sing of your strength,
in the morning I will sing of your love;
for you are my fortress,
my refuge in times of trouble.
Psalm 59:16

The Sovereign Lord is my strength;
he makes my feet like the feet of a deer,
he enables me to tread on the heights.
Habakkuk 3:19

For the message of the cross is foolishness to those who are perishing, but to us who are being saved it is the power of God.
1 Corinthians 1:18

It was not by their sword that they won the land,
nor did their arm bring them victory;
it was your right hand, your arm,
and the light of your face, for you loved them.
Psalm 44:3

But we have this treasure in earthen vessels, so that the surpassing greatness of the power will be of God and not from ourselves;
2 Corinthians 4:7

You are from God, little children, and have overcome them; because greater is He who is in you than he who is in the world.
1 John 4:4

Truly, truly, I say to you, he who believes in Me, the works that I do, he will do also; and greater works than these he will do; because I go to the Father.
John 14:12

Made in the USA
Columbia, SC
21 March 2023